Doris Stokes is a celebrated clairaudient who has confounded sceptics by the uncanny accuracy of her readings. In Australia she filled the Sydney Opera House and was mobbed in the streets. In America, 'Charlie's Angels' was removed from a prime television slot to make way for her. In this country her appearances on radio phone-ins have caused an avalanche of mail. In her first book, VOICES IN MY EAR, Doris told how she discovered in herself this extraordinary gift and how she has shared it with the world. In MORE VOICES IN MY EAR she continued her story and in INNOCENT VOICES IN MY EAR she told the story of her 'spirit children'.

She lives in London with her husband John and her son Terry.

Also by Doris Stokes (with Linda Dearsley)

DORIS STOKES
with Pam and Mike Kiddey

A Host of Voices

Futura

A Futura Book

First published in Great Britain in 1984
by Futura Publications, a Division of
Macdonald & Co (Publishers) Ltd
London & Sydney
Reprinted 1984 (twice)

ISBN 0 7088 2585 0

Typeset, printed and bound in Great Britain by
Hazell Watson & Viney Limited,
Member of the BPCC Group,
Aylesbury, Bucks

Futura Publications
A Division of
Macdonald & Co (Publishers) Ltd
Maxwell House
74 Worship Street
London EC2A 2EN
A BPCC plc Company

Chapter One

It looked as if someone had diverted the Thames and sent it down the Fulham Road. The rain was coming down in bucketfuls and everywhere was swimming in water. To make matters worse I was late for work and I'd just missed the bus.

But every cloud has a silver lining, even the big black ones that were now hovering overhead, and in the distance I saw a taxi driving towards me with its sign lit up. I flagged it down and scrambled into the back. 'Belgrave Square, please, and could you hurry? I'm late.'

I heaved a sigh of relief as I slumped back in the seat. And then I noticed the seat alongside me depress ever so slightly as if someone had sat down beside me. I realized that someone had, although nobody else would be able to see. Another spirit friend had popped in for a chat.

I'm afraid my first reaction wasn't very charitable. In fact I muttered, 'Oh blimey, please let me get to work first!' It had been a very trying morning. I'd been worried over the health of my husband John, he's an Arnhem veteran and hadn't been too well lately. The doctor had been hours late in coming to see him and by now I was supposed to be giving a demonstration of mediumship at the headquarters of the Spiritualist Association of Great Britain in Belgrave Square. I hate being late or letting people down so I was feeling really flustered and not in the best of moods. And yet it was obvious that somebody, or rather some spirit, wasn't prepared to wait until I got to work.

'Who are you and what do you want?' I asked.

A voice in my ear said, 'Tell Gerry it's Uncle Jim.'

'Who on earth is Gerry?'

The voice replied, rather abruptly I thought, 'The cabbie of course!'

I looked at the taxi driver, who had taken me at my word about hurrying. He was weaving in and out of the traffic like a racing driver. On a wet road too. I was terrified. The cab was rocking from side to side but I breathed in deeply, swallowed hard and then knocked on the partition window between us.

At first he ignored me so I knocked harder. He thought I was going to complain about his driving, but reluctantly he slid back the partition.

I said, 'Excuse me but are you Gerry?'

I could tell it wasn't what he was expecting. And in a voice that was more than a little surprised he replied, 'Yes! How on earth did you know?'

'Well,' I paused, licking my lips. It was me who now didn't know what to expect. 'I've got Uncle Jim with me here.'

The result was electrifying. Gerry slammed on the brakes and the cab skidded to a halt in a shower of spray and a chorus of angry hoots from other motorists. But Gerry ignored it all. He spun round and looked at the apparently empty seat beside me. Uncle Jim chuckled and said, 'Tell him I've got a message for Elsie, she's my missus.'

Gerry didn't hear this, of course. He was still staring blankly at the seat. Then he said in a voice shaking with a mixture of fear and bewilderment, 'What are you talking about, lady? We buried Uncle Jim last Friday!'

6

I ploughed on. 'He may have passed over but he's with us now and he's got a message for Elsie.'

'That's his widow,' squeaked Gerry.

'His missus actually, luv,' I said. 'But don't let's bring the whole of London's traffic to a standstill. Drive on and I'll find out what Uncle Jim has to say.'

The journey to Belgrave Square took twice as long as it would have done if I had waited for the next bus. Uncle Jim, in fact, didn't have a lot to say. His widow had been beside herself with grief and he merely wanted to reassure her that there was no need to worry and tell her not to mourn him. One day they would be reunited in the spirit world.

But although Uncle Jim's message was brief, Gerry had plenty to say. It was his first encounter with the spirit world and he wanted to know everything about it. It was obvious I couldn't tell him that much on such a short journey – I've spent my life as a spiritualist and I'm still learning – but at least by the time we parted company he didn't think I was mad. In fact Gerry was so grateful he refused to accept the fare for the trip.

As for myself it was nice to know that I had helped, not only by bringing comfort to a bereaved family but also by opening someone else's eyes to something that I regard as natural as living.

I know our little chat did have some effect because the next time I was giving a demonstration at the Spiritualist Association of Great Britain I glanced to the back of the audience and nearly fell off the stage with surprise. For not only was Gerry there, but the whole of the two back rows were occupied by great big burly cab drivers, arms folded, listening intently and all still wearing their licence badges on their lapels. What a heartwarming sight.

It confirmed something that I have become more and

more aware of since the publication of my first book four years* ago: that an ever increasing number of people want to understand not only what life is all about, but what there is *after* this life.

It was for this reason that I decided to spend the following twelve months touring the country, visiting towns and cities from Newcastle and Manchester in the north, through Birmingham to London, Ipswich and Southampton in the south and across to Bristol and Gloucester in the west.

We simply called each demonstration *An Evening With Doris Stokes* because that's what they were – just me sitting on a stage acting as a telephone exchange between the spirit world and its loved ones here on earth.

Memories of that tour are a mixture of hilarity and sadness. John and I made thousands of new friends from all walks of life. They were all so different, but there was always a common bond: everybody wanted to know about life on the other plane. Some were desperate to contact relatives who had passed over, so desperate, in fact, that they had almost lost the will to live themselves. Some were just curious. And there were a lot who were bewildered or just plain angry that a loved one had been taken from them in sometimes abrupt and cruel circumstances.

All these emotions I understand only too well, as readers of my earlier books will know. My own son John Michael was taken from me when he was just five months old. But even now, forty years later, I still suffer from twinges of sadness when his birthday approaches.

I still sometimes think: 'Dear God, if things had been

* Voices In My Ear

different I would now have grandchildren of my own.' But the loss of John Michael has helped me in other ways. And it has allowed me to help other people.

It encouraged me to develop a gift that I'd had – but not understood – since I was a child. I had tried a number of different religions and found most of them failed to offer me any real peace of mind or give me any reason to believe in an afterlife. But then I met a medium who showed me that my son was not lost for ever. I was given proof that he was alive and well and being looked after by his grandad in the spirit world. And my life changed. I went on to develop my own gifts and discovered that I was a natural medium. Looking back over the years, I pray that I have been able to bring the hope and comfort I received all that time ago to others in a similar predicament.

There is nothing really special about being a medium. Everybody possesses a third eye, not something you can actually see, but another sense. But developing this sense is rather like playing the piano. Some of us can do it better than others. Even so the gift of mediumship is no guarantee that life will always run smoothly and it doesn't help me to see into the future or perform miracles. Like any other gift from God it's something to be used with care and for the good of others. I wouldn't dream of trying to put it to any selfish use. And I'm absolutely certain that the spirit world wouldn't let me.

Some people think you've got to be specially intelligent to be a medium but I'd hardly call myself a mastermind. In fact there are times when I think I'd forget my head if it wasn't screwed into place. And there are other times when I have to laugh at the stupid things John and I have done. There were one or two

9

hilarious moments on our tour . . . like the time I was booked to appear at the Assembly Rooms in Derby.

The young man who had arranged the venue was called André. He was a partner in the company which had organized the whole tour and he was marvellous – very personable, very polite and attentive to our every need. Nothing was too much trouble and *almost* all of the time André was highly efficient.

I say *almost* because on the morning of our journey to Derby a normally unflappable André phoned me in a dreadful panic.

'We've got a terrible problem, Doris,' he said. 'I've ruined my contact lenses and I can't see a thing.'

The problem was, it was seven o'clock in the morning. The train left at nine. André didn't have either a spare pair of lenses, or a pair of glasses and there was no time for him to visit the optician. There *would* have been, of course, if he had let John and I travel to Derby on our own. But André wouldn't hear of it. He absolutely insisted on accompanying us in case we got lost. But since none of us had been to Derby before you can imagine it was rather like the blind leading the blind.

We managed to make it to the train on time and met André at the barrier. At least he could see well enough to find his way to the station! Our carriage was almost empty so I unpacked the sandwiches we had brought and over a picnic André explained the catastrophe of his contact lenses.

'I put them in a pan of boiling water to sterilize them, Doris,' he said. 'Then somebody phoned me and we were chatting for hours. In fact I forgot about them altogether. By the time I remembered, they'd boiled away to nothing!'

I was trying hard not to laugh but André didn't

mind. He had a sense of humour and could see the funny side of the story – even if he couldn't see anything else!

When we arrived at Derby station we stumbled off the train together and made our way to the nearest taxi rank. We didn't bother to ask the way to the hotel. André said we'd leave that to the taxi driver.

Unfortunately there wasn't a taxi in sight but it was a bright autumn morning so I didn't mind too much. Or at least I didn't mind for the first few minutes. But after a quarter-of-an-hour there was still no sign of a taxi and the three of us were starting to look a little forlorn. André was blinking blindly while I was stamping my feet to get rid of pins and needles.

Eventually I said, 'Look, we could be standing here for ever. You two keep your eyes on the luggage while I go and find some help.' Anything to get rid of those pins and needles. The men reluctantly agreed, although it did occur to me André wouldn't be a great deal of good keeping his eye on the luggage the way he was at the moment.

I looked up and down the street but there was still no taxi in sight. Not even a passer-by. Behind me was the station and a ticket barrier but there was no sign of life there either. I looked across the road towards a large building. It looked warm and inviting so I walked towards it and, peering more closely, I saw a sign which read *The Midland Hotel*. I hadn't walked more than a dozen odd steps so I called back to André, 'What's the name of the hotel we're staying in?'

'The Midland,' he replied.

I started to shake. And then I almost collapsed with laughter. So much for being able to see into the future. I was having a job seeing our hotel across the road!

So you can see that we mediums are only human

like anyone else, and sometimes we can be twice as daft. The spirit world will only help on really important matters. And even then only when it thinks it necessary. And it stands to reason: you can't have another dimension constantly interfering with our destiny. The future is what we make it.

A lot of people have asked why so many of the messages that I relay from the spirit world appear to be so simple. The answer is equally simple. These messages come sometimes as a signal, a guide, a clue or just a simple proof from a loved one who has passed over that there is another life hereafter.

When somebody passes over they don't change overnight. They don't suddenly possess a superbrain. They are the same people we knew here on earth and they are still concerned about the same sort of things. And I'm pleased that that's the way it is. I wouldn't like to think that they were no longer the people we used to know.

At every demonstration on tour we set aside time for a question and answer session which I hope solved a few mysteries about the spirit world but there will always be sceptics. An incident in Derby, for instance, typified the initial approach of a lot of journalists to *An Evening With Doris Stokes*. They just cannot believe that there isn't a catch.

We hadn't been in the Midland Hotel for more than a few minutes – in fact, John and I hadn't started to unpack – when there was a knock at André's door.

It was a reporter who apologized for intruding but his editor had set him a special assignment.

He had been instructed to shadow Doris Stokes from the moment she arrived in Derby until she went on stage at the Assembly Rooms. It was real James Bond stuff. André asked him exactly what he was looking for. And the young lad said anything, from friends being planted in the audience, informants combing the town for information and then telephoning it through, to spies eavesdropping on conversations in the bar at the Assembly Rooms. He even hinted that people could be so underhand as to slip notes to me under the door of the hotel bedroom.

The only phone call I did receive in that hotel bedroom, in fact, came from André who asked what he should do. I said, 'Bring him along and let him stay with us for as long as he likes.'

A few minutes later the reporter was ushered into our room and I watched as he glanced around curiously. I don't know if he was looking for hidden microphones or radios, but the only things he tripped over were the shoes that John and I had just kicked off to soothe our poor old feet. But we made him as welcome as we could, even though the bedroom did feel a little bit cramped with all of us in it. I was determined to let this lad prove to his editor that Doris Stokes had absolutely nothing to hide, at least not as far as being a medium was concerned!

Before every demonstration I like to have a little nap so that I can rest my body and my brain completely. Then I'll open up my mind and tune into any special or really urgent messages that might be coming through.

It *is* possible for me to be in *constant* communication with the other side, but I do tend to put my foot down and tell the spirit world, 'Look, please let me switch off now because I am just not physically capable of doing this twenty-four hours a day. I'm human and I need time like everybody else to wash the pots, peel the

13

spuds, look after my husband, go to the launderette and do the million and one other jobs to keep body and soul together.'

Normally the spirit world tries to respect my wishes, although I've learned I have to be firm because, just like the rest of us, it can be very pushy.

When I do tune in, the line is always very busy and that's why the wires occasionally get crossed and some of the messages are a bit confused. But on this particular day in Derby one message came over loud and clear. It was a young voice, very persistent and he kept telling me his name was Nicky. Maybe Nicky thought I might not be able to tune in properly because there was a reporter with me and he had to make a special effort. Whatever the reason, he came through loud and clear. Not only that, he had a musical accompaniment.

I said to John, 'You know, luv, I'm sure this Nicky died in a circus. I keep hearing fairground music.'

I was making a cup of tea when I heard the music and I reached for a teaspoon as I was speaking. But before I could dip it into the sugar basin, I felt my hand being guided towards the table.

My stomach was knotted with tension and my knees felt like jelly. I'm always like that before a demonstration but this time it was even worse as my hand spelled out the word MURDER. This had never happened before.

It shook me so much I shouted out loud, 'Come on, Nicky, that can't be right!' And then I heaved a sigh of relief as he came back to me again saying, 'No, no. You've got it wrong. My name is Nicholas Murden and I want to tell you my Daddy is coming tonight.'

The knots in my tummy untied themselves and I could feel the tension ebbing away. I sighed with relief.

14

Then I turned to John and the reporter and said, 'I think we're going to have a lovely evening.'

And we did.

Nicholas's father did turn up and was delighted to hear from his son. It was exactly one year since his little boy passed over and the circus was part of his address.

In his article the following week the reporter wrote:

> 'I suspect Doris Stokes can explain her gift of communication no better than Van Gogh could have detailed the chemical formula of his paints.'

I'm not quite sure what he meant by this, except that I think he finally accepted that the spirit world was prepared to speak to the people of Derby through me. And they were happy to do so without the aid of 007 type tricks.

The work I do and the way that it happens can be summed up in two words: love and harmony. And without those two vital ingredients it will never work.

I can't bring someone from the spirit world into contact with the earth plane unless there is some sort of bridge. There has to be a bond of affection which links them with someone here. I had to laugh when a journalist in Australia once asked me, 'Doris, tell me, what's it like to be able to raise the dead?'

I replied, 'I wouldn't know, son. I can't raise the dead. I couldn't even raise the skin off a rice pudding.' It really has nothing to do with raising the dead. That's a frightening phrase and it doesn't mean anything. We can all talk to loved ones who have passed on, but only if there is that bond. And where love and harmony do not exist it can be sometimes impossible to communicate any really meaningful message. This was something I learned in a very painful way at Stoke-on-Trent.

The day before John and I travelled to Stoke my promoter received one of those telephone calls from the police requesting my services. Somehow, although I never talk about them myself, they often leak out through enterprising crime reporters. And this one was no exception. The newspapers were full of the fact that I had been asked to help in another murder inquiry.

This time the call came from murder squad detectives in Leicestershire who were investigating the death of little Caroline Hogg. The poor darling had been abducted from her home in Scotland and was later found strangled alongside the A6 in Staffordshire.

I have helped in a number of murder inquiries in the past and I was only too willing to be called on again, but I have always found it a chilling experience.

The detectives came to our hotel bedroom shortly after we had arrived in Stoke and they handed me a photograph of the little girl. It had been taken a few months earlier. She was a beautiful, laughing child with dancing eyes and I immediately felt able to respond to her.

Through my mind flashed a picture of a layby, a wood, a field and a slip road. There were a host of other things, too. And they were flashing before me almost too quickly for me to be able to take them all in. I just kept talking, describing what I could see. And the words came tumbling out as I described in detail a place I had never visited but felt I knew so well. It was not somewhere I ever wanted to see again under any circumstances and, when I had finished describing what I had seen, I asked the senior detective, 'Where have I been?'

He replied, 'You've just described the place where we found the body. And you've described it in detail, almost down to the last blade of grass.'

I also provided one or two other pieces of information which produced something for the police to follow up, but no matter how hard I concentrated I was unable to get a clear picture of Caroline's killer. The reason for this was fairly simple. The little girl didn't know the monster who had taken her life. She felt neither love nor hate towards him on the earth plane and therefore there was no bridge through which to communicate. And that meant there were no details being communicated to me.

All I can do in cases such as this is give what leads or assistance I can to the police and hope and pray that the killer is eventually brought to justice.

Obviously the spirit world cannot pass on information on every wrong-doer; if it did we'd be in a right mess. Nobody would dare do anything without first looking over their shoulder. No, we've all been given a choice to make what we want of our own lives. I've always said we can either pass over with plenty in the bank of goodness or we can go over spiritually bankrupt. It's our own choice.

Chapter Two

Some years ago John and I decided that if we were really going to put the gifts that God had given us into action we would have to move closer to headquarters. I don't mean the office on the other side, I mean the Spiritualist Association of Great Britain. That's why we moved lock, stock and barrel from Lancaster to London.

The headquarters of the Association, which is known as the SAGB, is a beautiful 17th century house in Belgrave Square, London. It was designed by Sir Christopher Wren, but I shouldn't think for one minute that when he designed number 33 Belgrave Square he ever thought that one day it would be the home of the world's largest spiritualist association.

The SAGB is open every day of the week, including Saturday and Sunday, and mediums are in constant residence. You don't have to be a member, you can just pop in, but if you're after an appointment it's better to book in advance. Even the animals are not forgotten and every Monday there is a healing session for sick animals.

For we mediums it really is a lovely spot to work. It's steeped in history and there's a peaceful feel about the place, with most of the rooms exactly as they were the day the house was built. One of SAGB's most prized possessions is a grand elaborately carved arm chair which belonged to Sir Arthur Conan Doyle, who was a great spiritualist.

Sir Arthur is a former president of the Association

and we keep his chair in a room which has been named after him. There's another room dedicated to his friend Sir Oliver Lodge, a famous scientist and past president. So many interesting people have been members and become presidents or vice presidents of the Association. Some of them were born spiritualists and others, like the World War Two hero, Air Chief Marshal Lord Dowding, seeking proof of eternity, turned to spiritualism in later years. Lord Dowding like so many others thought the appalling waste of life during the last war was all so pointless, and felt that all those youngsters he had known could not completely disappear without trace, never to be heard of again. He could still feel their presence and was eventually successful in making contact with a lot of them.

You'll gather from what I've said that there really is a beautiful atmosphere in the SAGB building and John and I love being there. I'm only sorry that I'm not able to work there as often as I used to. My demonstrations are limited to one a month, but it's ever so nice to see so many eager friendly faces when I arrive. The biggest room in the building doesn't hold more than 200 people, which is one reason why demonstrations there seem so much more personal, it's just like one big happy family gathering. The intimate atmosphere certainly helps contacts from the other side come through very quickly. No sooner have I settled myself down than the blue lights are dancing all over the place. If the light is very faint or flickering I know that the soul hasn't been over very long. In the big halls where I've given demonstrations it's sometimes hard to see these newly passed over souls, but at SAGB they shine out like the precious gems that they are.

In fact their brilliance can be almost dazzling and they certainly know exactly where they want to be.

Kate, who came through at the SAGB meeting last spring, is a typical example of how this happens. Occasionally John will take his tape recorder along to a demonstration and afterwards we can both enjoy listening to all the messages again in our home. Fortunately when Kate came though, John had taken his machine and the following is from that tape. I saw a twinkling light dancing merrily in front of my eyes and then a young voice in my ear said: 'My name's Kate and I want to be with someone six rows back.'

I duly relayed the message and from a chair in the sixth row a man told me, 'That's my daughter spirit side!' I discovered later that this was Robert Parker, Kate's father. The contact continued as follows:

Doris: 'She went over very quickly.'
Mr Parker: 'Yes, she did.'
Doris: 'As I bring her in close to me I don't get any feeling of impact, which means that she didn't feel anything either. It was instantaneous. Who's Jason?'
Mr Parker: 'Jason was one of her boyfriends.'
Doris: 'I get a feeling I was thrown. Then there's nothing. Kate tells me that she was a long way from home and this is what upsets you. She says you're upset because you weren't there to say goodbye. She's sending her love to Chris. Who is Chris?'
Mr Parker: 'Her brother.'
Doris: 'She's also mentioned Alan and Dennis and sends her love to them too. She is also talking about a girl who I think is called Julie. Who is Julie?'
Mr Parker: 'Julie is the girl who died with her.'
Doris: 'Kate's also telling me that I've been where

she was. I'm going through my mind and I'm saying Melbourne, Sydney, Adelaide, Perth, Darwin and she laughed and said: "That's it!"

She also says that she was somewhere high up when this happened. It's the first time she's come through and she says, "I've tried so hard, I've wanted so much to contact my family and I'm so pleased that finally I have managed it."

At that point contact with Kate faded. As happens so often at SAGB lots of other souls were also trying to have their say, and to make any sense of their messages as they tumbled thick and fast into my ear I had to clear Kate's vibration. Short though Kate's visit was I'm glad she managed to get a message through to her father. Our spirit friends are just as anxious to make contact as we are to hear them. It is sad that there just isn't time to talk to all of them and the spirits must get just as disappointed and frustrated as we do. But it cheered me up no end to get the following letter a week after the SAGB demonstration.

Isleworth,
Middlesex.

Dear Doris,

To my great joy you reunited my daughter Kate and myself at your afternoon session in Belgrave Square. You will see from the enclosed newspaper report that you were absolutely right. The messages for Alan and Dennis you named were her closest university friends at Bath and another young English girl – as you said – passed over at the same time.

I hope you will not think this a sauce, but when I was at Belgrave Square, I noticed your husband

21

sitting under the portrait of Sir Oliver Lodge. Quite unconsciously he assumed the same position, chin resting on his hand and apart from the beard the resemblance between them is uncanny. They are almost doubles. May I suggest that you get him to sit under the portrait the next time you are there together and see for yourself!

Once again, my very deep thanks for your comforting messages from dear Kate.

Yours sincerely,
Robert Parker.

The newspaper cutting which Mr Parker enclosed showed a photograph of a beautiful young girl and the story began:

'A beautiful local girl has been killed in a road accident in Australia.

'Kathryn Parker died when the car in which she was a front seat passenger blew a tyre and crashed into a tree near Darwin, Australia. Another girl was killed in the accident and two others were injured . . .'

Mr Parker also enclosed a separate photograph of Kate for me to put in my Children's Corner, which I've done and he added a footnote to his letter which reads:

'I have joined a local spiritualist church and found great peace. I have never met a more balanced, peaceful crowd than fellow spiritualists and I am now wondering what my own contribution can be to repay some of the peace of mind I have discovered.'

*

It was the month after Kate had come through and once again I was leaving SAGB after a demonstration and was clutching a huge bouquet of flowers. They had been left anonymously for me on the stage and they really looked beautiful. I was just about to climb into a taxi when I heard someone say, 'I hope you like the flowers, Mrs Stokes.'

I turned round to see a sad-faced young man and from his eyes I could tell immediately that he had suffered a tremendous loss with which he had not yet come to terms. 'They really are some of the prettiest flowers I have seen for a long time,' I replied. 'Did you send them?'

'Yes, and there's something else I would like you to know. We were at your demonstration this afternoon and you brought our daughter through. We were so shocked and stunned we couldn't speak, it was as if we were paralysed, we just couldn't get the words out.'

I was about to ask who 'we' were when behind him I saw a slim young woman who, if anything looked even more distraught than her husband. I just had to help them if I could.

I was on my way home to our son Terry who wasn't well at all, in fact he'd had rather a nasty accident only two days previously and I was naturally anxious about him. But here were two desperate souls living daily in misery and torment and I found myself saying: 'Look, luvs, I've got to get home to see my son and although I can't promise anything, I will try to ring you as quickly as I can.'

It was the following day when I phoned them and that was how three days later Michael Welling and his wife Mary came to be sitting in our living room. They hadn't hesitated for a second when I told them I could manage a sitting for about half-an-hour. And it was

23

equally obvious that the object of their grief couldn't wait much longer to be reunited with Michael and Mary either.

No sooner had they sat down than a little girl, the image of her father, skipped into the room and ran straight to his side. She was a spirit child of course, but that did nothing to detract from the beaming smile she gave to her mummy and daddy.

'Your daughter's with us now,' I said. There was a look of astonishment and even a hint of disbelief on their faces, but I'm used to that and I carried on regardless. Now I was curious to know more about this lovely little child.

I asked the little girl: 'What's your name, luv?'

'Michelle,' she said.

I relayed the name and then the disbelief began to fade. I was just about to describe her and say how I admired her bright red hair when Michelle interrupted, 'Don't you dare say I've got red hair. And it's not ginger either. It's strawberry blonde.'

At this her mother gasped and tears welled up in her eyes as she said, 'Doris, that's just what she was always saying. Please, tell us, is she by herself or is there someone taking care of her?'

'Does the name Anderson mean anything to you?'

'Dear God! Yes, it does!'

'Peter Anderson?'

'Doris, he's my father!' And with that Mary Welling dissolved into tears of joy.

I wanted to know how Michelle, whom I took to be about eight or nine years old, had passed over. Her spirit grandfather explained, 'It's very upsetting, Doris. I'll send my little granddaughter away for a while and then I'll tell you.'

And he did. It had only been about three months

previously. Michelle was being treated to an evening at the local cinema with her parents. Ordinarily she would have been going along to the gymnasium with some of her friends, but a night at the cinema was an infinitely better idea. Excitedly she had skipped off to her friends to tell them she wouldn't be going with them.

Unfortunately she had decided to take a short cut which meant clambering over some spiked iron railings. Michelle slipped and one of those vicious spikes went straight through her heart.

'Believe me, Doris,' said her grandfather, 'she didn't feel a thing. I was with her when she passed over and her only recollection was one of falling. It came as a bit of a shock to find herself on the other side, but I'm looking after her. Tell Mike and Mary that she's in good hands. And do you know, the council were planning to move those damned railings the day after the accident.'

At that point Michelle came skipping back into the room and once more ran over to her daddy and kneeled beside him. She was such a beautiful child and although now there were no signs of the dreadful injury that had taken her over it was hard to understand at that precise moment why God had ever allowed it to happen. But then I looked at the faces of her parents, they had been transformed into expressions of pure joy. The bewilderment and the haunted looks had completely disappeared and I knew that now there would be no more periods of utter desolation. They knew that their little Michelle had not gone from them completely. She was here with us now and would always be close to those she loved so much here on earth.

It was at this point Michelle jumped to her feet again

and turned to me. She waved and said, ' 'Bye, Auntie Doris, thank you for talking to me and now Mummy and Daddy know I'll always love them won't they.' And with that she was gone but I know that she will be back again and so do Michael and Mary.

It was after this sitting that Mary in fact described her version of the events.

'The night before we went to the SAGB my husband looked at the photograph we've kept of our daughter and he said: "Michelle, if I don't get to speak to Doris Stokes, I just don't know what I'll do." He was so determined, or maybe desperate was a better word.

'We'd visited quite a few mediums but nobody had been able to help us overcome our grief or even provide us with evidence that Michelle had come through, or wanted to contact us.

'I have always believed in life after death. I know there is a place for us all when we leave this earth, but I'd never been involved in spiritualism. It's not the sort of thing that ever interested me. It's not the sort of thing many people would think about or would turn to, until they are hit by a tragedy as we were.

'When the first message came through from Michelle at the SAGB we were too stunned to do anything about it. Doris said she wanted to contact a taxi driver in the audience. That's Michael's job. But somebody else jumped to their feet. He was a driver and was also convinced that the message was for him. It became very confusing and later Doris said that she also realized that it was Michelle trying to come through to us.

'I never thought for one moment that we would

26

be able to get a private sitting and as for what happened, it's something I'll never forget. Doris was so accurate in everything she told us.

'I was convinced from the moment she described Michelle's hair. Both Michael and I are dark. Michelle took after her grandad. She was a true redhead but she insisted on calling herself a strawberry blonde. It was uncanny how Doris picked this up immediately. In fact at first I found it frightening, but then I realized that it was just our daughter talking to us. And who could be afraid of their own daughter? I'll never be afraid again and to know that Michelle is around us all the time is comforting and reassuring for us.

That sitting changed everything for us. Whenever I feel a bit depressed or upset now I just remind myself that Michelle is here. I know she's never very far away and in fact I can feel her presence and I know it's not just my imagination. Sometimes she even plays tricks just to let us know that she's with us. Only a couple of days after our sitting, I was vacuuming the carpet when the machine suddenly stopped. I went to see if I had accidentally pulled the plug out, but the machine had been switched off at the socket, I was alone in the house and plugs don't switch themselves off. I know who did it. It was the sort of prank Michelle used to play before that accident. It was her way of letting us know that she was still close to us – and up to her old tricks!'

Chapter Three

Never in my born days did I think I'd see the inside of Broadmoor and yet here we were calmly drinking tea and eating chocolate biscuits with one of the most notorious gangland killers in the country.

The visit was the result of a telephone call to our flat in Fulham one morning in September. I'd just struggled in laden down with the week's shopping when the phone rang.

'Answer that, luv,' I shouted to John as I juggled with carrier bags that were about to spill their contents out of the door and over the balcony. We live on the second floor and I'd visions of tinned beans plummeting 40 feet onto somebody's head.

'It's for you, Doris. Something to do with the Kray Twins.'

The remark was almost guaranteed to make me drop all the bags and rain down tins of food on every unfortunate passer-by within a half-mile radius.

Somehow I managed to put down the shopping before lunging for the telephone receiver. The Kray Twins? Like everybody else in London I'd heard of them. They'd been jailed fifteen years ago for a couple of particularly nasty murders, and terrifying stories of everything else they were supposed to have done while running a gangland empire were still rife. But what on earth had all this got to do with me, I wondered? Sounding a lot more confident than I felt, I said, 'Doris Stokes here. Can I help you?'

The voice at the other end of the line was friendly.

There was a hint of an East End accent but it didn't sound villainous.

'Sorry to bother you, Mrs Stokes, but I've got a message from Ronnie Kray. He wants to know if you'll visit him.'

I stepped back, and nearly fell over the shopping. A carrier bag toppled over, a tin was rolling out of the door but I managed to trap it with my foot, succeeding at the same time in almost dropping the receiver.

The voice asked, 'Are you there, Mrs Stokes? Did you hear what I said?'

'Yes. Hold on,' I said, performing contortions that I never thought possible. I kicked the tin back into the hall, nudged the front door closed and watched as the rest of the groceries spread themselves around my feet.

'Now then, where is this Mr Kray and why does he want to see me?' I was proud that my voice gave no hint of the drama that was being played out in our hall.

The voice at the other end of the phone, sounding just as calm, replied, 'He's in Broadmoor and he'd like to see if you can talk to his mum.'

It was one of the strangest requests I had ever received, but I had no hesitation in replying, 'Yes, of course, I'll see him. When would you like me to go?'

The voice said, 'Next Wednesday. We'll send a limousine for you. It'll be there 1 pm sharp.' And that's how the following week John and I found ourselves sitting in the back of an enormous chauffeur-driven car speeding along the M4 through Berkshire.

The 'voice', Laurie O'Leary's, was also with us. He turned out to be a very honest, well-mannered man, who had known the twins at school. They had gone their separate ways and Laurie had gone into showbiz management. After the jailing of the Kray Twins he

29

had become a regular visitor to both Ronnie and his brother Reggie who was in Parkhurst, the top security prison on the Isle of Wight.

Ronnie had read one of my books. Now he wanted to know more about spiritualism. He wanted to be convinced that there was a life after we pass over. And he wanted me to give him that proof. I had no hesitation in accepting the invitation because, whatever terrible things the Kray Twins had done, they were now being rightly punished by society and I believe it is wrong to deprive such people of any hope at all.

Broadmoor itself is a forbidding place, with huge electrically-operated steel doors sliding silently closed after you pass through them. No clanking of chains or echoing corridors but, of course, I was forgetting, it is a hospital for the mentally disturbed and not a prison – even if it is one of the most closely guarded buildings in Britain.

The silence was eerie and unexpected. But Ronnie Kray was an even bigger shock. We sat for about five minutes in a tiny, dingy reception room while our credentials were checked. Then we went into the visitor's lounge.

There were six tables scattered around a large room, which was rather shabby and reminded me of a works canteen. All the tables were occupied by people in civilian clothes so making it hard to tell visitors and patients apart. But one man sat alone at the table nearest to the door. He was immaculately dressed in a beautifully-tailored brown suit, white silk shirt, highly polished shoes and a gold watch that twinkled under the harsh lights. His dark hair, going grey at the temples, had been cut very stylishly. I thought to myself, 'If this was a works canteen, that would be the managing director.'

Then he rose from the chair, held out his hand and said, 'Doris, I'm so grateful you could come. I'm Ron.'

Before I had time to reply he was alongside me, pulling back a chair and ushering me into it. He clicked his hands towards a young man in a white jacket and said, 'Bring a selection of biscuits. Or would you prefer a hot meat pie, Doris? Tea? Coffee? Cigarette?'

It was almost too much. We settled for tea and biscuits and then, almost immediately, a voice said to me: 'I'm glad he hasn't let himself go. I brought my boys up to be clean and tidy.'

It was one of the quickest contacts I had ever made. Mrs Violet Kray was obviously anxious to help her son so I said, 'Ron, your mum's also with us.'

At first it didn't register with him. Like most people when I first meet them, Ron expected me to either go into a trance, speak in a funny voice or at least make some ghostly noises.

To prove his mum was there I added, 'She says she's met someone called George. They used to run a market stall together.'

Ron Kray, the gangland killer, began to tremble. He whispered, 'That's right, they did.'

Then Violet started nattering to me saying, 'Their Dad only left £500 you know.' I repeated it aloud and Ron nearly fell off his chair.

'That's right, absolutely right, the exact amount.' There were tears in his eyes. He grabbed my arm and said, 'That's the proof I need.'

But there was more to come, 'I know it wasn't a lot but I didn't need money. The boys always looked after us.' That was Mr Kray senior.

Then it was Violet's turn again. She gave me the

31

name of the hospital ward in which she died and told me in detail of the two rings she had left her eldest son, Charlie. She said she now wanted the twins to wear one each on a chain round their necks.

It was all happening so quickly and, although the voices in my ear were loud and clear, I was speaking in not much more than a whisper. I was oblivious to what was going on around us.

Violet was really in full flow by now. 'I passed over just before our wedding anniversary. I never got over losing the twins. I put on a brave face but I never got over losing them. I had a broken heart, I blamed myself for what happened and every night I asked myself where I had gone wrong.'

Then she insisted I speak direct to Ron and tell him, 'I'm happy you never tried to take yourself over, you could have but you didn't. Keep your chin up and one day you'll be reunited with Reggie on the earth plane. You're paying for your crimes and taking it in a way that makes me proud.'

By now there were tears streaming down Ron's cheeks, but they turned to tears of laughter when Violet added, 'I was a bit upset about my teeth. Remember, I got some new ones just before I went over? If I'd known what was going to happen I'd have saved the bloody money!'

The voice faded. It was a perfect exit line from a woman who had known an awful lot of heartache in this life and yet had faced it with cheerful good humour.

It was then Ron's turn to open his heart to me. We talked on for almost another hour, 'I'm not moaning about my sentence nor asking for a reduction,' he said.

'I'm not pretending that these days I'm an angel, but

I am turning to God. And it's happening *despite* the "do-gooders", not because of them.

'I'm grateful to you, Doris, because you came to see me today and you haven't preached at me once.'

Ron paused and flicked a speck of cigarette ash from that immaculate suit.

I commented, 'You look like an executive in that outfit.'

He smiled and replied, 'You've got to keep your self-respect. It's the only thing that keeps you going. Or at least it was until today.'

I sensed it was time to go. Other prisoners had been keeping a respectful distance from us, but now as we rose from our seats the young man in the white coat who had been serving the tea came forward.

'You're Doris Stokes, aren't you?' he said. 'I came to see you on stage when I was a little boy. My mum will never believe I've met you. Just wait till I tell her.'

He looked so fresh, his face wasn't yet lined with the cares of the world. What on earth was he doing in a place like this, I wondered.

Ron Kray must have known what I was thinking, because as soon as the youngster had gone he said quietly, 'Doesn't seem the type to be a killer, does he? But he is. In for life.'

Then he handed me a box of the sweetest and most delicate lace handkerchiefs I have ever seen, kissed me lightly on the cheek and said quietly, 'Please, please come and see me again one day.'

I walked out through those huge top security steel doors and into the autumn sunlight. I breathed in the fresh air deeply. It had been a shattering experience. Where are we going wrong when fresh-faced youngsters convicted of the most terrible crimes are in a place like that?

The limousine was waiting. The chauffeur opened the door. And there on the back seat was a beautiful bouquet of red roses with a note attached:

'From your friend, Ron. Thank you, thank you.'

I climbed in, scooped up the bouquet and sank back into the plush upholstery. I felt moved to tears.

How he had managed to get hold of the lovely handkerchiefs and the flowers in Broadmoor I shall never know, although it seems that as it is a hospital rather than a prison inmates *are* allowed certain privileges. But I was truly touched. Whatever he had done – and he *is* serving a recommended minimum of twenty-five years in prison – I had seen another, gentler, side to the infamous Ronnie Kray.

I thought back over our conversation. Together with the sitting, it had lasted for almost two hours. Never once in that time had Ron tried to whitewash his past in any way. He'd told me: 'I did what I did and now I'm paying the penalty. I'm not complaining.'

The nearest he had come to any sort of excuse was to say, 'Innocent people never got hurt. We only tangled with villains.' That was no excuse, of course, but by his gestures and his thoughtful gifts he had proved to me he was still a human being capable of feeling. If nothing else, I like to feel that our meeting had brought him some sort of hope and faith with which to face the long years ahead behind those walls.

It was dark by the time we got back to Fulham. The lights in our block of flats were twinkling, warm and welcoming. No sooner had we put the key in the door than the phone was ringing. It was my friend Nancy from down the street.

'Where've you been, Doris? 'I've been trying to get you all afternoon,' she said.

I was tired after the journey and without thinking I replied: 'Nowhere special really, Nancy, only Broadmoor.'

There was a pause at the other end of the phone, then Nancy said, 'Well, fancy that!'

'Yes, Nancy, fancy,' I said. 'But I must go now. I'm dying for a cuppa, luv.' I didn't want to talk. There were so many things I didn't understand. I felt it was time to sit back and think over my impressions of the day: Ronnie, his mum, the eager childlike face of the young murderer. The twilight world of gangsters and killers was alien to me and yet I could warm to the generosity of Ronnie Kray. I kicked off my shoes and went into the kitchen to fill the kettle.

Every night before I go to sleep I meditate and, more often than not, Ramonov, my spirit guide, is there to offer help and advice. This evening was no exception.

As I lay alone on the settee, his voice and his clear wisdom came through to me, 'You're worried over something that doesn't concern you. You were right to visit but you must never try to judge.'

Chapter Four

The gang of punks standing in the queue at the booking office of the Odeon Theatre in Birmingham were enough to frighten the life out of anybody. Hair the colours of the rainbow, dangling chains, black leather and safety pins everywhere except where they should have been – which is on a baby's nappy as far as I'm concerned.

The local paper had just announced that the singer, Boy George, was going to appear at the Odeon and pandemonium had broken out. Everybody wanted tickets. I was due to appear at the same theatre a week later and it was a friend of mine, Ed Doolan of the BBC, who told me the story.

His girl friend was standing behind these punks in the queue, waiting to collect a couple of tickets that I'd left for my sitting. Never having seen such characters close up before, she was fascinated, and more than a little bit apprehensive. 'It wasn't so much that they were aggressive,' she explained later, 'but with those spiky haircuts and all those chains they looked terrifying.'

But the biggest shock came when they finally elbowed their way to the front of the queue and told the girl behind the counter, 'Seven tickets for Doris Stokes, please.'

A year ago I might have been equally surprised. But early on in our tour I began to notice the increasing number of young people in the audience wherever I went. They weren't just sitting there silently. And they hadn't come to sneer either. They genuinely wanted to know what was in store for us all.

It is a trend which always brings me fresh hope. With unemployment and crime and drug abuse, I sometimes think the world's in a dreadful state but if these youngsters are willing to come and listen to a pensioner, and if there's a chance of me offering them a better sense of the future then I feel that what I am doing is worthwhile.

And it has been, every single minute. I loved working with these young people. There's nothing like it to keep both body and mind alert.

There have been times though, I must confess, when I've been flummoxed for a minute or two by what they've said. It happened for the first time when I was appearing at the Corn Exchange in Ipswich.

The first part of the evening had gone extremely well. I had been fortunate enough to be able to put a couple in touch with their son who had been tragically killed in a motorcycle accident and to brighten up another young woman's life by passing on messages from her father. She wasn't entirely convinced – until I told her exactly how much money Dad had kept in his cigar box!

There were 900 people in the Corn Exchange, filled to capacity, and everybody wanted to be put in touch with somebody. Or else they wanted to ask a question.

The hardest thing about these demonstrations is that it just isn't possible to help every single person. If you were one of the disappointed ones on this tour I hope you'll understand. But the object was not to contact individual loved ones. It was to demonstrate through contact that there is life when we pass over.

The second half of the programme always opens with a question and answer session where I try to answer general questions relating to my beliefs. I came out on stage to find a line of people standing in front of me. And not one of them could have been over twenty-one. It looked more like a fashion parade than an evening with Doris Stokes! But I was delighted.

The first young lady stepped forward, looked me straight in the eye and said, 'Doris, is there relations in the next life?'

'Well, of course, my luv, you'll see all your relations,' I replied.

She giggled and said, 'Nah, I don't mean *them* relations. I mean sex. 'Cos if there isn't, I don't think I wanna go!'

Now how do you answer that one! The rest of the audience roared with laughter. And they clapped even louder when I said, 'I'm not sure, darling. I've got past the stage when I ask that sort of question, but all I pray is that you don't go over till you're too old to worry about it!'

She was a charming girl and in actual fact very serious about her question. There was no smuttiness involved, just a genuine and honest enquiry. And it took some guts to stand up in front of nearly 1,000 people to ask what a lot of other people must have been thinking.

The simple answer, I believe, is that there is no 'sex' as we know it here on the earth plane, but there is a tremendous amount of love, so much so that we have no need for such earthly pleasures.

A lady asked me on another occasion, 'What'll happen to me, Doris? I was my old man's second wife. He was a widower and now he's up there. Is he with her and what happens when I pass over? Which one of us will he choose?'

This is a very common worry and the answer is that

on the other side there is no possessiveness. In the spirit world there is no jealousy but a life of harmony so there's no question of choosing one partner or another. If you have lived a rich and happy life together on earth it will continue in the spirit world.

Another question which sometimes causes a lot of sleepless nights, especially among younger people, is what happens when a baby goes back to the spirit world before it is born? Are the parents ever blamed for it's death?

Even before the baby is conceived the spirit world has chosen parents and a guide for the new child. So if the spirit world reclaims it before it reaches the earth plane it will be cared for, named and grow like any other child. And it will know nothing but love for its true parents with whom it will eventually be reunited. My heart goes out to every parent who has lost a child before birth, but rest assured that the spirit world will love your children as much as you would.

Some of the questions, though equally important, are on a different level. Such as: do animals have an after life too?

Well, animals are definitely psychic and there are many instances of pets coming back to say hello to families they left behind. So there's every chance you'll meet up again when you pass over.

Actually I know I'll be meeting up with a wonderful pet we had called Matey. She was an affectionate, but very independent, tabbycat. And she certainly shocked the local vet on one memorable occasion.

We'd just moved to London and the flat was in chaos with packing cases half-empty all over the floor. I didn't know where to find anything. Except the cat. And you couldn't miss Matey. She was squawking loud enough to be heard in the next street. At first I thought it was just because she was upset over moving. But when the caterwauling went on for over an hour, I realized it must be something serious.

I picked her up in my arms and stumbled backwards and forwards across a lounge that looked like a battlefield. Every other step I broke a plate or bent a knife but it did no good. Matey kept squawking.

Eventually I had a brainwave. Why not ask up above if anyone could tell me what was wrong with Matey. So I did. And back came the answer: 'She's got toothache!' So I telephoned the vet. The number was handy, as always. In fact it goes into my personal telephone book before I even look up the address of the doctor.

I'm sure to this day the poor girl on the reception desk must think she was on some kind of Candid Camera. The conversation went like this;

'Hello, is that the vet?'

'Yes, who's speaking please?

'You don't know me but I can assure you that you come highly recommended.'

'What's the problem?'

'It's the cat. She's got toothache.'

'How do you know?'

'The spirit people told me.'

There was a pause, then she blurted out, 'I'll tell the vet and he'll be round as soon as possible.'

Within an hour there was a knock at the door and absent-mindedly I called out, 'Come in, Peter.'

It was the vet. 'How on earth did you know my name?' he asked. Then a look of near-panic came over his face and he said, 'Who told you? Not the same people who diagnosed toothache in the cat?'

'Of course,' I replied. And to add to his bewilderment the spirit people's diagnosis proved to be right as well!

*

John was busy packing his shaving gear into his holdall when I shouted to him: 'Which tent shall I take this time?'

'Let's have the green one with a few instant flowers growing up the side,' he replied. 'But don't spend too long making up you mind or we'll miss the train.'

The tents are the nickname John gave to the flowing oversize gowns I wear on stage. I wear them, not for effect but for comfort. It gets very hot under the spotlights and the false boob I've worn since my mastectomy doesn't make it any easier.

I was in the bedroom frantically trying to push the tent into an already overcrowded suitcase in between leaving notes for Terry, the milkman, the lady who comes in to try and keep us tidy and Nancy who keeps a watchful eye on the flat. John meanwhile had lost his cufflinks yet again and the place was in general uproar as it always is when we're setting out for a venue.

This time our destination was Leicester and I was looking forward to the trip because I hadn't visited the city since I was a young woman. Somehow I managed to cram everything into the case and with John bouncing up and down on the lid I even locked it as well.

Every time I packed on this tour I thought back to the upheaval there used to be when I was a little girl as we got ourselves ready for the annual week's holiday in Mablethorpe or Skegness.

In those days the preparations began weeks in advance and for days before we went away we all had to wear our oldest clothes while our best were being washed, ironed and aired ready for the big day.

I often wonder what my mother thinks as she looks down from the other side and sees just how easy it is to pack today with all the non-crease materials around. She used to spend endless hours trying to keep us clean

41

but it wasn't time wasted. Everything looked lovely when it had been crisply starched with labours of love. Mum used to run herself ragged after everybody. She was no intellectual and she had no other skills except her one great ambition which was to look after everybody around her as best she could. And she used to achieve that ambition every day of her life, God Bless Her.

But if we had to put the same preparations into going away these days I don't think John and I would ever get out of London so I suppose every age has its compensations one way or another. John and I always like to travel light but I'm only human and I do like to look my best when I'm on stage. It's also important that I feel relaxed. I'm a bit of a fidget at the best of times and having been chopped about a bit over the past few years my poor old body does play me up now and again. I can't be doing with anything tight or restricting around me which is why those huge tents I wear are ideal. They also help to hide a figure which is a bit more lopsided than it used to be a few years ago! At the same time I'm glad to say that what's left of me is more or less in one piece and I'm happy to make the best of it. And that's just what I try to do.

There may be a hair or two out of place from time to time but I'm not one for spending hours in front of a mirror before I go on stage. In fact if we're staying away overnight I try to get my hair set in Fulham before we go.

If we're away for more than a couple of days it can present a few problems because I don't like going to strange hairdressers. It's not quite the same as at home where you can feel at ease and be yourself. Quite often the hotel will recommend a hairdresser who will come up to the room which I like because then we can have a good old chinwag. There was one hotel, and to spare and blushes I won't mention the town, where one of the waitresses offered to loan me her own heated rollers.

I said, 'That's very sweet of you, luv. Thanks very much.' And I was even more grateful when she offered to put them in for me. An hour later I was sitting in an armchair with most of the rollers safely installed and chatting away happily to the young lass when a voice came into my ear.

'Tell her I know it will all work out, Doris.'

'Who are you?' I asked.

'I'm Martha. Do you like the ring she's wearing? Tell her she's got a fine boy and I know the ring will bring a lot more happiness to her than the other one.'

Of course the young waitress couldn't have known about this conversation. She was chatting away happily about last night's telly but she noticed I'd suddenly gone very quiet and asked anxiously: 'Are you all right, Mrs Stokes, is anything the matter?

'I'm fine, dear,' I said. 'But tell me, who's Martha?'

'Why that's my fiancée's mother. She passed over last year.'

I didn't know how to put the next question. Martha had said, 'Tell her the ring will bring her a lot more happiness than the other one.'

Did that mean the young lass had been married before?

I doubted it. In fact she looked hardly old enough to be eligible for the first time around. As tactfully as I could I said to her: 'Are there two rings involved somewhere, luv?'

It's a phrase I use. I never in public ask anyone, or rather, tell them I know they have been divorced. I'll say 'they tell me there are two rings' or maybe 'They tell me you've taken one ring off and put another one

43

on.' If the sitter wants to elaborate it's up to them.

But there was genuine bewilderment on this young girl's face.

'There's only one ring as far as I know, Mrs Stokes. I don't understand what you mean.'

I breathed in deeply and thought: 'You've started now, Doris, you'll have to finish girl.' So I said, 'Martha says the ring you're wearing will bring a lot more happiness to you than the other one.'

The puzzled look vanished and she burst into laughter and blushed at the same time.

'Ooooh! That's a bit embarrassing but I'll let you into a secret, Mrs Stokes. My fiancée was engaged before but they broke off. This is the ring he gave her. We thought we might as well use it as we need to save every penny we can for a new home. But you can tell Martha thanks for the message and I'll certainly try to make her son happier than he ever could have been with the girl who jilted him.'

It's a funny old world, isn't it? And it's even funnier, some of the things you learn when you're having your hair done!

The one thing I really like about staying in hotels, apart from not having to do the washing up, is that I can have a bath whenever I like without being disturbed. At least that's what I used to think but that little dream was rudely shattered on our visit to Leicester.

We had been booked into a very swish modern hotel right near the centre of Leicester and the staff couldn't have made us more welcome but as usual everything was one mad rush. No sooner had we booked in than I had to dash off to the local radio station for a phone-in programme. I think the presenter was a bit disappointed that I didn't have two heads and that I talked like any other ordinary human being but the programme was a great success and the questions came in thick and fast. We were on the air for almost an hour and as I slumped into the taxi taking us back to the hotel I said to John, 'I know exactly what I'm going to do now. I'm going to have a nice hot bath, then I'm going to put my robe on and have a nap.'

I had it all planned out. What a relaxing way to spend an afternoon. Especially an afternoon like this one. It was wintertime and there was a sharp frost in the air. Inside the hotel there were warm rooms with warm towels – and that warm bath. But I'd hardly sank into the bubbles when an almighty clanging sound startled me out of my wits. I almost swallowed some bubbles with fright. Then I realized what it was. The fire alarm! The next thing I heard was John thumping on the bathroom door shouting: 'Come on, luv. Out of there quickly. We've got to get down the stairs!'

I leaped out of the bath, grabbed a towel and wrapped it round me, then threw open the bathroom door.

I stopped dead in my tracks. John by this time had opened the bedroom door and I could see all sorts of people scurrying down the corridor. Then I heard sirens. The fire brigade had arrived. But I stopped dead in my tracks; I'd forgotten something.

'What's the matter, Doris, come on, let's get moving.' John still had the door held wide open although everybody outside was in too much of a hurry to notice us.

'Close that door a minute, John,' I said as calmly as I could. 'Help me find my boob. I'm not going out there until I put it on.' Like any other woman who's had a mastectomy I can feel a bit self conscious at times and fire or no fire I wasn't going out without my false boob.

John's face was a picture, I don't think he knew whether to laugh or cry. 'Forget it.'

'I won't! And don't just stand there. Close that door and help me find it. Please, John, it's important to me.'

By this time I was galloping round the room, dripping water all over the place, and frantically pulling everything out of the wardrobe. John sighed and dropped to his knees. He was still looking under the bed when they announced that everyone could go back to their rooms. It had been a false alarm. John was a gem. He didn't lose his temper at all but I learned something from that episode. From that day on I always keep my extra padding somewhere where I can grab hold of it quickly in emergency.

And of course it did happen again, this time in Manchester. I wasn't in the bath on this occasion but I was wearing my nightie and robe when the alarm sounded. Calmly I slipped on my boob and we walked out into the corridor.

I must admit that having gone through this sort of panic once we felt like old professionals and just a bit superior. We headed towards a door marked 'Fire Exit' and it must have been our almost casual approach to it all that made this foreigner want to join us. Poor lamb, he looked so bewildered and couldn't speak a word of English. He was jabbering away in a language that neither John nor I understood so John just said to him, 'Come with us, mate, tag on behind.' And he waved his hand towards the emergency door. At least the stranger understood that bit. He clutched hold of the back of John's jacket and hung on for dear life as we walked down and down and down those stairs.

We must have gone down seven flights of stairs when I finally sat down puffing and panting. I just couldn't go on and I said so.

'That's it, John, my head's spinning like a top and I'm not going another inch. If my time's up I'm going here and now where I'm sitting.' The foreign gentleman, still clutching onto John's jacket just nodded and smiled as if he understood every word.

At that moment a door opposite opened and a voice said: 'Why, it's Mrs Stokes, please come in. Would you like a cup of tea?'

'What about the fire?' I asked.

'Oh don't worry. Somebody set the alarm off accidentally.' And we were still supping tea fifteen minutes later with the hotel's head chef when the general manager walked in and told us, 'You are honoured, Mr and Mrs Stokes. Nobody is ever normally invited into Chef's office for tea.'

'Honoured or not, and it's all very nice, but how are we going to get back up to our room? I can't possibly face all those stairs again,' I said.

It was Chef who provided the solution, 'We'll send you back up in the service lift.' And they did, along with the clean linen and towels and the foreigner who still hadn't left us.

As we got out of the lift I said to him, 'That's it. It's all over now. You can go back to your room.'

He was looking puzzled.

I said: 'Fini. It's fini.'

'Fini?'

'Yes, fini!'

'Aha, fini!' He was looking triumphant. At least he had understood something. He threw his arms round me, plonked a big kiss on my cheek and said, 'Bye-bye.' Then he walked off down the corridor. I often wonder if he ever knew quite what was happening, especially when they bundled us into that lift with all the washing! As for myself I made another rule after that episode. From that day on I have always warned hotel staff that fire bells seem to have an uncanny knack of going off when we're around. To save everybody a lot of time and trouble and to save me having to scramble into my boob would they please let me know, when the alarm goes off, whether it is a real emergency or just another fault.

Chapter Five

With thirteen cancer operations under my belt plus a mastectomy I've long since come to treat every day as if it might be my last. My old friend Dick Emery used to joke: 'The spirit world must want you badly, Doris girl. They're trying to take you over bit by bit!' It's all very well to treat every day as your last but when there's so much more work to do there's no point in knocking yourself out before the bell goes!

It was in the autumn of last year that the doctor confirmed my suspicions. My mastectomy was playing me up and I was ordered to hospital for tests. Sadly I had to cancel appearances in Southampton and Brighton. The tickets had already all been sold and I felt dejected but there was nothing else I could do.

So there I was, tucked up in my hospital bed, feeling sorry for all the people I'd disappointed and, I have to admit, more than a little bit sorry for myself. I was beginning to wonder what on earth I was doing being miserable in hospital when I could be just as miserable at home. In fact I'd decided to get myself home if I had to go by dustcart when the memory of my meeting with a dear old lady, Mrs Fox, came flooding back.

It happened while I was in a convalescence home after my original mastectomy operation. It was a gloomy afternoon and I was feeling really fed up with myself, staring out at the rain streaming down the window pane.

Behind me I heard a voice ask, 'Is it raining very hard?' I didn't turn round, which I knew was very rude of me but I was in a right mood. I thought to myself, 'Well, can't she see for herself what a lousy afternoon it is?'

Still staring out of the window, I said, 'Absolutely bucketing down.'

The voice replied, 'Oh what a shame for you. Aren't I lucky? I see only what I want to see, so for me it's a lovely, bright day out there.'

I spun round and saw a little old lady painfully holding herself upright on two sticks. I realized to my horror that she was blind. How could I have been so rude, wallowing in my own self pity.

She must have sensed my embarrassment because she said, 'I used to have sight, and because of that I have lots of beautiful memories. So now, whatever the weather, I can look at what I choose. I think that's very lucky, don't you?'

At that moment I felt so humble I almost felt like kissing that old lady's feet. What a wonderful outlook on life! It taught me a lesson I've never forgotten, or at least a lesson of which I constantly remind myself. No matter how badly off you think you are, there's always somebody in a worse state.

Looking back I'm certain it was Ramonov who actually arranged that embarrassing interlude in the convalescence home. It would be one of his lessons, like a parable from the Bible except that Ramonov's lessons sometimes come in the form of shock treatment. One thing is certain, they're lessons one never forgets! And they can act as a tonic – I was beginning to feel better already. Not well enough to get back into the hectic round of touring but certainly fit enough to get back to my household duties. So I was allowed back home.

I was about to hop out of bed the next morning when the doorbell rang, so I dived back under the covers and left it to John. There was a muffled conversation and then I heard my gallant husband exclaim, 'Hurry out here, Doris! Look what's arrived.' I peered around the bedroom door and couldn't believe the sight that met my eyes.

It was a man from the local florist's shop carrying the biggest bouquet of flowers I'd ever seen. It was like one of those huge bunches they give a singer at the end of an opera or an actress when she's just finished playing in a Shakespeare drama and everybody stands up and applauds. The only difference was that I can't sing opera or recite Shakespeare and a flat in Fulham isn't a West End stage. In fact, at that moment I couldn't do anything. I was speechless. There was a card with the flowers which said simply: *Get Well Soon, Doris. With Love.* And that was it. No name, no address and no one I could thank – except the man from the florist's. I just burst into tears. And he beat a hasty retreat.

Half-an-hour later he was back with another bunch and again there was an anonymous note. By the end of the day there were enough flowers to set up a rival business to the florist's down the road. As if he could read my mind, John joked, 'The place is beginning to look like Covent Garden – and I don't mean the opera house.' Almost all the flowers had arrived anonymously, but I discovered the majority had come from the Southampton and Brighton areas where notices had gone up saying my appearances were cancelled due to illness.

It was wonderful! People are so kind. I'd let them down and they were sending me bouquets! There and then I resolved that whatever happened I would make it to Brighton and Southampton one day and it was going to be in the not-too-distant future.

*

Actually the enforced rest was really a blessing in disguise. It meant that I could do some catching up on the mountains of letters that were pouring in. Normally I get a flood of hundreds every week, but once I had started the tour this flood turned into an avalanche of thousands. A lot of them don't need answering. Some are merely poems or prayers that people send because they know I will like them, and others are heartbreaking letters brimming over with almost irreconcilable grief from people who just can't come to terms with losing a loved one. I have this recurring nightmare that one day someone will turn to me and pour out their heart and when they don't receive an immediate reply feel rejected and do something drastic. Please God, it hasn't happened yet, and I can only say that every letter eventually gets read but it does all take time. So please, please if you are one of those who've written, bear with me and if it is humanly possible there will be a reply.

I rarely reply to personal criticism because I do feel we are all entitled to our own beliefs, but there are occasions when criticism can't go unanswered. For instance, a Birmingham vicar once wrote after one of my appearances:

> 'It is sad when the bereaved consult a medium and all too often it is the most recently bereaved who go to hear mediums. It is sad to think that help is sought in this way.'

Naturally a lot of bereaved people do come to me seeking assurance that one day they will be reunited with their loved ones. And it's a fact that a lot of people don't start thinking about the after-life until they find it looming up on them, or someone close passes over.

But for the vicar and those of you who believe there is something wrong in consulting a medium, I'd say that the word 'medium' means mediator, and that it has always been my belief that we all find our *own* way to God, be it with the established or alternative Churches, or totally independently.

Chapter Six

Our home is crowded with all sorts of souvenirs. There is first and foremost my corner for the spirit children. It's not so much a corner these days though, it takes up almost one whole wall of the lounge and it's growing every week as I get more and more photographs. There's a cuddly Koala bear to remind me of Australia and the time we went to the Sydney Opera House and there's a painting which art experts might describe as being primitive. I suppose it is but I think it's lovely because it was painted specially for me with love by a man whose daughter I helped to contact. It doesn't match the wallpaper, of course, and it clashes with the curtains, but who cares? To me it's an important work of art.

Among all the other bric-à-brac there's also a beautiful cut-glass goblet. It's so delicate I'm scared to drink out of it so it just stands there on the mantelpiece. There's an inscription on it in ever so tiny writing – I don't know how they managed it – but it really is beautiful and it reads:

Doris Stokes, Thank you for a sell-out performance at the Civic Theatre, Halifax. September 17th, 1983.

It was given to me by the Manager of the Civic Theatre, Mr Robbie Robinson, who has since become a great friend. I have to say that I'm proud the theatre was full that evening, who wouldn't be? But I was surprised nevertheless. It was my first visit to Halifax and I didn't really know what to expect.

Halifax is a Yorkshire mill town with its roots buried deep in the days of the industrial revolution, when poor little mites had to go to work almost before they could walk. But if you think it's all mills and shawls then you'd be completely wrong. I didn't even see a single clog! In fact I felt quite at home in Halifax. There was a happy, relaxed atmosphere and a genuine warmth in the greeting. Maybe I felt at home because it wasn't far from Grantham where I'd been brought up and where we'd had our own share of hard times in my childhood. Or maybe it was because, like Yorkshire folk, I'm prepared to call a spade a spade and not a so-and-so shovel. Whatever the reason, I liked Halifax. Even so I wasn't quite prepared for the welcome we got.

Sitting in the dressing room, I was unaware of the build up in the audience. As always, I was concentrating on tuning in, waiting for the voices to see what messages the spirit people wanted to give their loved ones that night. Not an easy thing to do I can assure you when your heart's pounding like a drum, your mouth's as dry as the Sahara Desert and you're shaking like a newly-made jelly. In other words, I was feeling just as I normally do before going on stage.

But the moment I walked out onto the stage, I felt that atmosphere laden with love and goodwill and the nerves disappeared. I asked how many people had actually seen me before and there was no more than a handful. The majority, in fact, hadn't even been to a medium before so straight away I put them in the picture. 'I don't go into a trance and you won't see apparitions in white sheets going "whoooooo" and floating round the theatre. In fact you won't see

55

anything unusual at all. Because what I do is quite natural. We just chat with the spirit world. I can't demand that they come, that's up to them. I can't dictate what they say but if it is likely to cause embarrassment I won't pass it on in public – unless you want me to.' There was a roar of laughter, a voice was already calling in my ear and I knew we were in for a lovely evening. The messages came thick and fast and as usual there were a few tears – though always, I hope, tears of joy.

There were, however, quite a few looks of bewilderment when I asked, 'Who do Derek and Arthur belong to? Derek has only just gone over to the other side.' Naturally enough quite a few people in the audience had relatives with those names, they're common enough, but there was no one who fitted into the pattern I'd described. And yet throughout the evening those names kept coming through. I could tell that Derek had passed over very recently. It was he who was giving me both names. His voice was urgent, almost frantic, and it was obvious that he desperately wanted to talk to someone.

Half-a-dozen times I pleaded, 'Come on, someone knows Derek and Arthur. I know they do.' I didn't add that Derek's voice was verging on the hysterical because I didn't want to upset anyone. But there was no doubt in my mind that he was a very distressed soul and that somehow his fate was inextricably bound up with that of Arthur's. They weren't brothers, of that I was convinced, but until someone had accepted them here in the audience there was nothing more I could discover. Or so I thought. Derek desperately wanted to talk to somebody, but there was obviously no one here in Halifax willing to take a message.

I was disappointed and more than a bit puzzled.

Why should Derek be so insistent? It was a long time since I'd heard such a disturbed voice. After the session I half expected a knock at the dressing-room door and someone apologizing, 'Sorry, Doris, they were for me. I was just too stunned to stand up when you came out with them in the theatre.'

It's something that happens quite frequently although I'm constantly asking people to speak up as soon as they think I've got a message for them. It doesn't bother me if they don't but it's frustrating for the spirit people who are trying to make contact.

But this night in Halifax the only knock at the dressing-room door came from the Manager, Robbie Robinson. He was beaming all over his face and in his hand was that beautiful cut glass goblet. It was already engraved. He'd known the evening was a sell-out – the 'house full' notices had gone up a week before – but he hadn't told me. Thank goodness, I'd have been even more nervous. Robbie said, 'Wonderful evening, Doris, marvellous. I've never known such an atmosphere in this theatre before. All those happy faces.' He thrust the goblet into my hand saying, 'What else can I get you?'

As usual after a sitting, I felt like a wet rag, completely drained and exhausted. But I knew what I'd like, 'I'd love a cup of tea, luv.'

Robbie almost fell over with laughter. He turned to John and said, 'Incredible. Pop stars who only bring in half an audience demand champagne and all your missus wants is a cuppa. We'll make it a pot.'

We all had a laugh, but at the back of my mind I was still bothered by those two names and was still waiting for that embarrassed knock at the door. It never came.

We drove back to the hotel and a supper of beef sandwiches, cheese, pickles and a pot of tea. Not the best meal for your digestive system late at night! It was almost dawn before I managed to fall into some sort of sleep and the last thing I remembered was a voice calling, 'Doris, Doris.' It was Derek. But it wasn't until four days later and two hundred miles away that I solved the mystery and heard from him again . . .

I don't know how the Romans felt when they marched into Gloucester a couple of thousand years ago, but my first visit was something I'll never forget. I was due to appear at the Leisure Centre, and John and I decided that we'd travel down the day before to get a good night's rest before the demonstration.

We set off for the West Country – and what a lovely run it is. In fact I was so engrossed in the scenery I forgot all about the snoozing I'd decided to do. The countryside is beautiful at any time of the year, but in autumn I think Mother Nature wants to let you see one big final splash of colour before she pulls the winter blanket over everything. Just a reminder that'll stay with you through until spring. And for me it always does, but this time there was the added bonus of seeing it all in a completely new setting. And I was enjoying every moment of it. I was just thinking how nice it would be if some of the council flats in Fulham could have been built of Cotswold stone, when my daydreams were rudely interrupted by a voice I thought could have been heard from one end of the carriage to the other.

It almost screamed at me, 'Here, Doris, here! This is where I lived. Please stop. I'm so ashamed at what I did. I just couldn't live with myself. I'm sorry, truly sorry! I know I shouldn't have done it.'

I recognized the voice straight away. It was Derek.

And he was alone. There was no mention of nor murmur from Arthur. But what to do? My first instinct was to reach up and pull the communication cord. In fact I was halfway to my feet when I suddenly thought, 'Steady on, Stokes. If you stop the train what are you going to tell the guard? There's a spirit person in distress? He might believe you but the chances are that he wouldn't.' There was a fair chance that, far from appearing at the Leisure Centre, I'd be appearing before the local magistrate!

I'd no idea where we were at that moment – although I discovered later we'd been on the fringes of the Forest of Dean. The carriage was nearly empty but jumping to my feet had woken John up. He blinked at me and said anxiously, 'What's the matter, girl, you feeling all right? You've gone as white as a sheet.'

I was trembling, I knew that. But it had been a shock for a voice to come through so urgently, and at a time when I was just relaxing and enjoying the scenery. It had given me quite a severe jolt.

'I'm all right, luv,' I said as I eased myself back into the seat. 'It's nothing to worry about.' But I was worried. There was obviously a spirit who wanted to talk to me urgently.

The train was slowing down now. I strained my ears but Derek didn't return. I glanced out of the window as the train pulled to a halt. We'd arrived in Gloucester, a lovely town steeped in history and old world charm. It was hard to imagine that I hadn't been dreaming. But it wasn't a dream, of that I was certain. I could only hope that Derek would come through again and tell me what was troubling him.

The hotel we'd been booked into was a lovely place just outside the town and overlooking the Severn Valley. The view was breathtaking and you could look right across the valley to Wales on the other side. It was once an old country house with huge thick Cotswold stone walls with ivy climbing up them to add to the rustic atmosphere. A maid led us up to our room on the first floor and almost before I'd plonked my handbag down, I sensed another old bit of atmosphere. 'You've got a ghost here, haven't you?' I asked the maid.

I thought she was going to faint! She spun round and looked at me in astonishment, and then almost as if she was frightened she gasped, 'How on earth did you know that?'

'Oh, don't worry, luv. I can just tell, but we're not going to pack our bags and gallop off.'

'Well, it's true. It's the ghost of a man who died in the room above you. Some say he committed suicide a hundred years ago,' she told us. Then she added, almost in a whisper, 'I don't talk about it much. People think you're daft if you do. I haven't actually seen him, but I know he's around. I'm really not imagining things.'

I knew she wasn't. I could feel his presence as soon as I had walked into the room, but just as I was getting ready to sit and find out more about him the telephone rang. A young lady from the local paper. Could she please come and see me before the demonstration? Of course, I always welcome the press. And at least she wasn't demanding to trail me round from the moment I stepped off the train!

When she did arrive we had a nice little chat but although she subsequently said some nice things about me, I could tell she was very sceptical. But then most journalists are.

On the off chance, I asked her, 'Do the names Arthur and Derek mean anything to you? I'm not sure but I think they both died quite suddenly. It could have been a road accident, but I don't know any more at the moment.'

There was a pause but after some thought she decided the names meant nothing to her. So I'd drawn another blank. We finished the interview, the young lady promising to come along to the demonstration the following evening, and said our goodbyes.

I decided to have an early night, after all that was why we'd come down a day early – to make sure I was relaxed and ready. John walked out into the hotel garden with me and we both watched as the sun disappeared over the Welsh hills in the distance. It was a marvellous sight, something you don't see down the Fulham Road! So peaceful and calm. Beneath us we could see over the whole of the city of Gloucester and beyond was the River Severn, gliding gently on its way to the Bristol Channel.

Water normally has a soothing effect on me, but not this evening. Somewhere out there everything hadn't been as tranquil as it looked. I wished I knew why, but no voices came to offer me an explanation. It was beginning to get chilly. John took my hand and said, 'Come on, luv, let's get inside. I know there's something bothering you because you're miles away. Sleep on it and maybe you'll find the answer by morning.' If only it was so simple! I took his advice anyway, but the only spirit that came through was the ghost who'd died in the room above.

It was late in the night when the tapping started. At first I thought it must be John tossing and turning, perhaps in a restless sleep he was banging the bedhead. But when I turned round, there he was sleeping like a newborn babe.

Then I heard a chuckle and realized – it was the

ghost. Actually I don't like using the word 'ghost' because it always conjures up images of someone floating round in a white sheet which is just plain silly. What they are are spirits who haven't moved on to a higher plane for a variety of reasons. Sometimes, especially if they died violently, they just won't accept that they are dead. Sometimes, if for example they've been badly wronged – and plenty of poor souls *have* been over the centuries – they simply want someone to know that they protest their innocence. This one, I somehow felt, had no axe to grind. Certainly he had no intention of harming anyone. He was just a little bit lost – and had been for a hundred years or so! He'd come to old Doris for a bit of advice.

I sat bolt upright in bed and said very sternly, 'Come on now, hop it! You've already passed over. No more silly games, you're on your way to higher things and the sooner you realize it the sooner we mortals can get a good night's sleep.' It worked. The tapping stopped and there were no more chuckles. He accepted that it was time to move on – and I said a little prayer to help him on his way.

How do I know that he had gone? It's nothing tangible, nothing I can point to. I can only say I knew it the same way I knew before I asked the maid that there was a ghost in the hotel. I glanced across at John. He was still fast asleep. It was almost two o'clock in the morning. So much for my early night in bed!

Actually, the following morning I wasn't feeling as tired as I had expected. Maybe the clean Gloucestershire air was acting like a tonic – and perhaps being able to help a spirit on his journey also contributed. However, as the day wore on I began to feel a little apprehensive about the evening demonstration. It was an odd sensation, and something I hadn't experienced before on this tour.

The Leisure Centre is a fine building in the town centre with all mod cons and aids to health and recreation, but I was feeling far from relaxed when I walked in through the back door.

Out front it was a hive of excitement and activity as the collapsible chairs filled with people. Nothing out of the ordinary. So why the apprehension?

I thought of doing the unheard of and peeping behind the curtains to see if there might be any reason for all this anxiety. Then I took myself in hand: 'Stokes, your brain must have gone on holiday. What on earth do you think you're doing?

'What's the first thing you tell people when they come to a demonstration? You tell them if they expect to see Doris Stokes swing from the lightbulb or hear ghostly voices then they're going to be disappointed.'

Quite right too. And yet here I was thinking of peeping out from behind a curtain looking for some sort of celestial sign like a wave from the angels. At that moment I heard a voice say, 'And now ladies and gentlemen, I'd like you all to give a warm welcome to Doris Stokes.'

It brought me back to earth with such a bump I nearly tripped over my evening dress. Instinctively, I grabbed the curtain for support. I have to admit I'm no fairy when it comes to weight, and for an awful second or two I thought I was going to bring the stage curtains down on top of us all. What an undignified start to the evening *that* would have been! But the angels, or rather the spirit guides, must have been on hand to look after me. There was a slight groaning sound from somewhere near the ceiling but everything held in place, I

63

regained my composure and walked out to my seat at the centre of the stage.

The warmth and love that came up from the hall with the applause made me realize how foolish my fears were, I was among friends, some of whom had travelled many miles. It was up to me to bring them what hope or comfort I could. I could tell immediately from the love I felt that tonight the telephone exchange between us and the spirit world would be busy. And it was.

That night in Gloucester the messages came through thick and fast. Then, after about an hour, I thought I'd try for an answer to the question that had been niggling me for some days now. I asked, 'Is there anyone here who knows Derek or Arthur? They were friends who died suddenly. They may have died together, but I'm asking because they came to me last week in Halifax. Is there anyone here with connections in Halifax?'

No-one took up the lead. In front of me were rows and rows of faces with that sympathetic but 'sorry I can't help' look. Then very, very faintly a voice came to me and I said suddenly, 'I know one of them was called Bourne or Horne or something like that.'

A young girl in the centre of the hall stood up and I thought, 'At last, a reaction.'

Then she said, 'I think it could have been Derek Thorne. It was in the paper some time ago. He was a murderer. He killed the other man.'

Suddenly I felt sick, my stomach turned over. I didn't know if I'd heard right. I'd thought they were friends, so I said, 'I'm sorry, my luv, I didn't quite catch that, What did you say?'

She repeated it and added, 'Thorne was recently found dead in his car but he committed the murder a long time ago.'

So that was it! But there was no point in dwelling on it here and now. I couldn't hear anything more from either Derek or Arthur, although I was sure it must have been one of them who had just come through with the surname. But there was apparently nobody in the Leisure Centre prepared to receive messages from them so communication was made impossible. I made a mental reservation to get hold of that paper as soon as possible.

It was nearly midnight before John and I got back to the hotel, laden down with flowers, photographs and greeting cards with messages that brought a lump to my throat. I started reading them and it always heartens me to realize that with so much heartache and trouble in the world there is still room for so much love. But it had been a long and emotionally exhausting day. I placed the flowers in the vases which the hotel had thoughtfully supplied, then I piled all those messages neatly on the dressing-table and resolved to finish reading them all first thing in the morning. I would also be calling in at the local newspaper office.

In the event I had no need to. John woke me up with a pot of tea and a back number of the local newspaper. I've still got that paper and a story on the front page reads as follows:

'A Forest of Dean man convicted of murder fourteen years ago has been found dead only a few miles from the scene of the killing.

'A senior police spokesman at the County police headquarters in Cheltenham confirmed this morning that Derek Thorne, who was found dead near Speech House in a car on Friday was the Derek Edward Thorne convicted of murdering Arthur Thomas Hogg in 1969.

65

'Mr Thorne was found dead in a car with the engine still running and police said there were no suspicious circumstances.

'The murder, in August 1969, of British Rail van driver Arthur Thomas Hogg at home near Parkend and the subsequent six-day trial caught the imagination of the public in the Forest of Dean.

'Mr Thorne was convicted on a majority 10-2 verdict by a jury at Monmouthshire Assizes at Newport and sentenced to life imprisonment.

'After his release from prison it is understood he married and moved to the Bristol area to live.

'During the trial, the prosecution led by Mr Brian Gibbens QC, assisted by Mr H. Woolf, alleged Mr Thorne who was 20 and described at the trial as being of no fixed address, lay in wait at Mr Hogg's home and shot him from a bedroom window as Mr Hogg stood near the front door when he returned.

'They said he then took Mr Hogg's money, went to Newport where he bought a car and travelled to Dingwall, Scotland, where he was arrested some days after the body was found. Mr Thorne was defended by Mr Alun Davies QC, with Mr Desmond Perrot. The defence contended Mr Thorne had been staying with Mr Hogg and was in bed when Mr Hogg returned home.

'When he returned Mr Hogg wanted to have a homosexual relationship which Mr Thorne refused.

'Following a fight, inside and outside the cottage, Mr Thorne shot Mr Hogg with Mr Hogg's own shotgun in self-defence.

'The scene of the murder, Howbeach Cottages, was demolished some twelve years ago.'

I read through that report again and again, each time with a growing sense of sadness. No-one can condone violence, let alone the taking of life, but I found myself pitying Derek Thorne. What he had done was without doubt wicked, but he had spent years in prison for his crime.

As far as society was concerned he had paid the penalty, but it was obviously not enough for Derek himself. Throughout those years in a prison cell he had been wracked with guilt.

I thought of that voice and what it had said to me: 'I'm so ashamed at what I did . . . I just couldn't live with myself . . . I'm sorry . . . truly sorry . . .' And I cried. Then I prayed, fervently, and for a long time, for that poor soul who had obviously been compelled to take his own life.

No-one should ever condemn anyone who commits suicide. I know for sure that they're not punished in the after life but rather cared for. People driven to such desperate measures are mentally ill, in much the same way as others are physically ill. And when they pass over they are nursed back to health again.

So why then did I receive that call, that plea and that apology? I believe that after ending his life and passing over Derek was temporarily lost, in the sense that he was unsure of what steps to take on the other side. He wanted comfort and guidance. Until he received it his earthbound soul was likely to stay in the vicinity of his crime and death.

Guidance is something that comes from God, but we can all comfort spirits and help them with our prayers which is why in Gloucester that morning I prayed as hard as I possibly could. And I know my prayers were answered because since that day I've not heard from either Derek or Arthur, nor have I felt in the slightest bit troubled about Derek's progression on the other side.

Time is something which has no meaning when we leave this world so I can't say how long it takes to nurse anyone back to health on the other side. But, as a former nurse, I can tell you that in our hospitals on the earth plane the greatest thing you can offer a patient near to the end of their life and with no hope of recovery is TLC – Tender Loving Care – and it's what nurses offer in abundance when no medicine on earth is going to make a patient better. And believe me it isn't given in vain. Tender Loving Care helps enormously in nursing someone over *to* the other side, and it is also something given to patients *on* the other side where it restores them to perfect health.

I was given a fleeting glimpse of life on the other side by my son John Michael.* He was just a baby when he left me and a strapping handsome man of thirty-six when he returned to take me on a visit to the spirit world. I met my mum who, on the earth plane, had been blind in one eye and yet her sight had now been restored to perfection. John Michael showed me one of their hospitals, set in idyllic scenery where you could feel the air vibrating with healing power. I asked my baby, or rather my now grown-up handsome son, 'Why do you need hospitals over here if you lose all your infirmities when you come over?'

He told me, 'Well, you see, when a person leaves a body very quickly, especially through violence, a car accident or maybe a heart attack, they haven't had time to prepare themselves, and it can in that case be a very

* See *Voices In My Ear*

traumatic experience. They come here to recuperate and, surrounded by their loved ones, they sleep until their spirit body recovers from the shock.'

If it was only a dream, as some have suggested, I can only say it remains as vivid today as when it happened several years ago.

It's the same for those who are exceptionally unhappy, as in the case of poor Derek. He too would remain in hospital, receiving lots of TLC until he is fully recovered. And once safely tucked up in a spirit hospital bed there would be no need to contact Doris again! I know that prayer had guided him through the doors of that hospital and that one day Derek and I and so many others will come face to face and have a good old natter!

Chapter Seven

Mystical music and flowing robes have never played a part in my life as a medium. Apart from anything else, I'd feel a proper Charlie dressed up like that, and secondly it might just look a little bit out of place in Fulham Broadway on a Saturday morning! I've never used crystal balls, tea leaves or playing cards either, but they can be useful to someone who is just learning mediumship. No one actually 'reads' tea leaves, of course, and no matter how long you gaze into a crystal ball you won't physically see anything. But they are handy as props, something on which to concentrate or focus the mind. Eventually, as a medium becomes more proficient, he or she should find they can manage without such props, but it may take some time.

The nearest I ever got to flowing robes and music was when John and I were invited to spend a weekend with a religious sect at their headquarters in Norfolk. It was a huge mansion set in its own grounds, and the people who lived there wore orange robes and called themselves disciples. (Their leader, whose name I never learned to pronounce, came from India, I believe.) I had been invited to give a demonstration of mediumship as part of their first ever open week-end for the public.

The people I met there were gentle, honest and hard-working, but as soon as we were shown to our bedroom, I said to John, 'I can't stay here. I'm off in the morning.' It was, to say the least, very spartan. There wasn't even a proper bed, just a mattress lying on the floor, and on the walls someone had painted huge sunflowers. Lying on the floor, you felt as if you were in some nightmarish jungle. It wasn't the sort of wallpaper I'd have chosen for our flat, and that's an understatement!

To cap it all, there wasn't even a chair to sit on, just a pile of cushions and a very low coffee table. I looked around in dismay and told John, 'If I get down on that lot to eat I'll never be able to get up again.' But that's how the meals were served: You were supposed to sit cross-legged in front of the coffee table! It was hopeless, of course, and I was ready to repack the bags and leave straight away, but fortunately John found another room with a window-ledge. That was where we ate, standing up!

The first night's evening meal was marvellous. We had chicken with plenty of fresh vegetables, and I later discovered the people who lived there grew all their own food. As I stood against the window-ledge, plate in front of me, looking out, across the flat Norfolk countryside, I thought, 'Well, it's not too bad and we're only here for a couple of nights, so let's make the most of it.'

Then another visitor popped her head round the door and said, 'Enjoy your dinner because it's the last one you'll get. I've just heard that from tomorrow we're on a diet of raw vegetables and yoghurt.'

For the second time in less than an hour I was ready to pack my bags – until John pointed out we wouldn't be able to get a train until the morning anyway. I tucked into the chicken as if it really was the last meal I was ever going to eat and then, literally, fell into bed!

The following morning, with a back that was aching more than I thought possible, I hobbled along the corridor to the reception area where I saw a nice, young man in one of those flowing orange robes.

'I admire your principles and the way you spurn all modern luxuries,' I told him, 'but honestly, I'm too long in the tooth for it. Please can I have a proper bed tonight, or else I'm afraid I'll have to leave.'

He looked at me in astonishment. I could tell they weren't used to my sort in this place and he was probably thinking, 'Got a right one here, expecting the four star hotel treatment.' But I didn't care. I just wasn't going to spend another night in agony.

Fortunately, I didn't have to wait for his reply. I hadn't noticed, but standing behind me was the head cook and bottle-washer. I heard a voice say, 'Of course, Mrs Stokes, anything you want.' I spun round and saw a very attractive young lady with laughing eyes. And I could tell she was having a job to keep her face straight.

Then she said, 'We'll put you and your husband in the healing wing. We've got what you call proper beds in there.'

They had and it was sheer luxury. Real tables and chairs, as well. John and I were almost envious of the facilities they had in that sanctuary. Apart from every comfort for patients, there were some first class special tables for massage – and not a painted sunflower in sight! It was all very restful.

We discovered that Jane, the head cook and bottle-washer had trained as a solicitor but had given up everything to join the sect. I've never seen anyone work so hard. She used to get up at two o'clock in the morning to mix the dough for the bread and then snatch an hour's sleep before she started baking the day's supply.

But although she was a disciple, she hadn't lost her

sense of humour. She whispered to me, 'Come up to my room if you don't like raw vegetables and yoghurt. I'll cook you a proper meal.'

Her room was equipped with every mod con, including a very fancy stove and Jane, noticed my look of surprise as we walked through the door. She said hastily, 'Oh, please don't think I'm doing anything behind anyone's back. It's just that Mum comes to visit us sometimes and all this is for her.'

'She wouldn't come if I didn't guarantee her what she calls *proper* meals.'

Jane's mother was obviously a very sensible woman. She even brought her own folding deck chair in the boot of her car!

Moving into that healing sanctuary gave us a really peaceful three days. In fact, John and I liked it so much we went back again for a complete week's rest and we were made very welcome by the disciples. Mind you, there were some embarrassing moments. For instance, the washrooms didn't have proper doors. They were like those things you see in a Wild West saloon on the telly which swing backwards and forwards with huge gaps at the top and bottom.

And I'll never forget the sight that greeted me when I looked out of the window one morning. It was raining and a dozen disciples were racing across the grass towards the main entrance. They'd hitched their orange robes up way above their knees to get a bit of speed up and stop their clothes from being dragged in the mud. As they sped past me, their garments flapping in the wind, I noticed something else and I couldn't help giggling at the rear view.

John asked in astonishment. 'What's so funny, luv?'

'Nothing really,' I giggled. 'But I bet this lot get a bit

cold in the wintertime. They don't wear any underpants!'

My demonstration on mediumship – and, of course, that was why I had been invited – went very well indeed. Many of the people there had never seen me before, but they made me feel very much at home and when there is a feeling of harmony it always makes it easier for the voices in my ear to come through.

We all sat in a big hall with a small stage at one end – and, for once, there was a proper chair for me to sit on. I looked down the hall and remember saying, 'I want to be somewhere near the back.'

'I've got a message for someone who lives in Blackpool.' Then I added, 'Whoever it is lives in Stanley Street, Blackpool.' A voice piped up and said, 'That's where I live, Doris.' It belonged to a young man with a round, cherubic face, very smartly dressed and wearing a bow tie. I'd never seen him in my life before but I said, 'The message comes from Beryl.'

He replied, 'Yes, yes, that'll be my Auntie Beryl, she's only recently passed over.'

'Well,' I replied, 'she's telling you to persevere, don't give up, and above all don't feel disheartened. It will all work out.'

The young man told me that in fact he was an astrologist, an occupation which was hardly guaranteed to bring him a steady income, and at times he had felt like packing it all in.

I replied, almost without realising what I was saying, 'Keep at it. I promise you within the next two or three years you will find yourself in demand both in the theatre and on television.'

Predictions are not normally in my line and even now I don't know what prompted me to say that with

74

such conviction. Maybe it wasn't really me at all, but Auntie Beryl trying to encourage her nephew.

What I do know is that the young man has become a firm friend of mine and whenever we meet he reminds me of what I said that weekend in Norfolk. His name is Russell Grant and now, of course, following his colossal success on breakfast television, he is one of the most famous astrologers in the country.

*

I was gently snoozing. Not quite awake and yet not really asleep when I suddenly had that strange feeling that somebody had slipped into the room. It wasn't a scarey feeling, there was no danger, but I opened just one eye rather slowly all the same. And there he was standing by the window with his arms folded and looking over at me. The uniform was smartly pressed and he wore his cap at a jaunty angle over a pair of twinkling eyes. 'Good Lord, it's Ginger Flanagan,' I gasped.

He laughed: 'Yes, Doris, it seems ages since we met.'

'It's not that long,' I said. 'Anyway how are things?'

'Well,' he said, moving closer to the middle of the room, 'the wife's moved into a new home and she seems to have settled down nicely but I still like to keep my eye on her and if you see her I'd like you to give her my love.'

Before I had time to ask for the new address Merchant Seaman 'Ginger' Flanagan had disappeared as quickly and as silently as he had arrived. Or had I just dreamed that he was there? Certainly I was quite alone now in this hotel room. It was in Chatham, a town with a long naval tradition but I knew for certain this wasn't Ginger Flanagan's home ground.

It was about a year ago when we had first met. We

were introduced in a manner of speaking by Ginger's wife, Anita. Her world had fallen apart when Ginger had been killed in the Falklands. He was one of those brave men who died on board the *Atlantic Conveyor*, merchant seamen who had volunteered to sail into battle with the Royal Navy. Ginger had come through me to comfort his wife and give her the will to live on. He had in fact done even more as Anita admits herself.

Anita went on to fight for better compensation terms on behalf of all the Falklands widows and she had become something of a national celebrity although we hadn't met again since that sitting. I was still trying to work out why Ginger should have paid this surprise visit when I dozed off again.

Three hours later I was on stage at the Central Hall, Chatham. It used to be a Methodist church and had a nice cosy atmosphere which was matched by the audience. They were friendly and receptive. And there's no doubt that this creates an environment which encourages contact with the other side.

One of the first spirit people to come through was Doreen White who told me she was a mother of three who had passed over twelve months earlier. She'd come to say hello to one of her former workmates, Yvonne Wilkinson, who was in the audience.

Doreen told me confidentially, 'I was big like you, Doris. But I was a big fool too. I let my size worry me. Don't you make the same mistake as I did.'

I relayed this message to Yvonne and told her, 'I don't really understand all this, luv, but I hope it makes sense to you.' Even as I was speaking I could hear a gasp go round the hall and realized that it must have been of some importance.

Then Doreen chuckled in my ear and said, 'Pass on

my love to Gwen and Veronica too. We used to work together round a long table you know.'

She relayed several other messages and told me her husband had given her a red rose. He wasn't in fact in the audience that evening but confirmed later that he used to send Doreen a red rose on special occasions.

Doreen's voice faded and I moved on to another contact with absolutely no idea about the controversy I had stirred up but it was all over the front pages of the evening papers the next day.

I was given some inkling during the interval when John heard somebody mutter: 'She's read about that case. She couldn't possibly have come out with all that otherwise.'

I was so angry I demanded to know exactly who Doreen had been and in the second half of the programme I began by saying that I had heard the criticism and the accusations and denied them categorically. I know there was no need for me to deny it but remarks like that are really wounding.

The following day I discovered, reading those front page reports of our meeting, that Doreen in fact had died after being prescribed a course of slimming pills by a local doctor. An inquest which had received considerable local publicity two weeks earlier, had returned an open verdict.

I was pleased that her friend Yvonne had told reporters I had mentioned facts which had never appeared in any newspaper – including the names of her workmates. It also cleared up another little mystery for me – why Doreen had mentioned the long table round which they all worked. It might have been a trivial fact but it was accurate and the sort of detail that would have been known only to her friends and workmates.

Another little mystery was also cleared up as John and I sat in the dressing-room after that demonstration. There was a knock on the door and one of the members of the hall staff popped his head round to tell us an old friend was dying to meet us.

He ushered in a cheerful dark-haired young woman who's face was vaguely familiar. At first I couldn't put a name to it then it dawned on me.

'You're Ginger Flanagan's wife!

'What on earth are you doing in this part of the world?'

A grin broke across her face from ear to ear. 'Well, Doris, I've moved into the area and when I heard you were appearing tonight I just had to come along.'

So that was why Ginger had come through in the afternoon. He knew Anita would be at the theatre and he had tuned into me while I was relaxing. I just hadn't taken the hint. I was now more than a bit upset, especially for Anita. But if I know Ginger it won't be too long before he pays another visit and next time I'll be prepared. But it just goes to show that mediums are as human as anyone else. We can all make mistakes can't we?

Chapter Eight

The little lad looked lovely. He had a mop of blond curls and was dressed in his Sunday best. There wasn't a hint of shyness as he dashed up and down the aisle, totally ignoring the thousand or so people who were crowded into the Town Hall. He shouted to me, 'Look at my hair now, Doris. It's nice, isn't it? Just like it used to be. And I feel really good. It's all so exciting.' Still nobody in the audience took any notice of him, but it was hardly surprising. The little lad was a spirit child.

I'd never met him before but it was obvious he'd come this evening to contact someone. I said to him, 'Yes, your hair does look smart and so does your suit. What's your name, luv?'

'Stephen,' he said, and then dashed up the aisle at the side of the hall shouting: 'Over here, Doris, come on over here. This is where I want to be.' And he disappeared behind a row of seats.

I pointed over to that corner of the hall and said, 'I know I want to be around there. Is there anyone sitting there who has a little boy called Stephen in the spirit world?'

Stephen prompted me. 'Tell them about my hair, Doris, and how nice it looks. It was all tufty when they last saw it. They'd like it now.'

I realized what the little lamb was telling me, so I added, 'The little boy I'm talking about probably died of cancer and was given a lot of treatment in hospital.'

A middle-aged woman jumped to her feet and said,

79

'We know him, Doris. We nursed him when he had leukaemia.'

Stephen whispered, 'That's right, they're the ones I've come to see. They nursed me for ages but eventually I had to go. Tell them to pass a message on to Mum. Tell her not to worry. Everything's fine and please, please tell Mummy about my hair.'

I duly relayed the message, and it transpired that the radium treatment Stephen had received in hospital had caused a lot of his hair to fall out. But here, in Hanley Town Hall near Stoke-on-Trent, he'd come back with a bouncing mop of curls that would make any mother proud.

Stephen's parents' last impression of him would have been of a poor little mite with little or no hair, so he wanted them to know that he was well again, and as bonny a young lad as he had ever been. And that sort of message means more to a parent than a million carefully chosen words of comfort.

The couple that Stephen had come to see were in fact healers. They were also spiritualists, and they had given both healing to Stephen and spiritual comfort to his mother during the little lad's ordeal. They hadn't come specifically hoping for a message from Stephen and they were most surprised when he popped up to say 'hello'. I'm sure when they went back to Stephen's mother, that message would be something for her to treasure for the rest of her days. And the knowledge that he was restored to his handsome good looks and energetic ways will, I'm sure, sustain her throughout the years until they are together again.

Certainly Stephen's mum would have received more comfort inside the Town Hall than from the group of religious fanatics who spent the evening on the steps outside. They were preaching Hellfire and damnation for anyone who dared spend an evening with Doris Stokes.

It saddens me that some people feel this way. Spiritualism isn't something to be afraid of. If you're afraid of any religion there's something wrong. Perhaps one of the great advantages that we mediums have is that most of us can laugh at ourselves, we don't need other people to point fun at us. I always like to tell the joke about the time a sports fan went for a sitting.

He told the medium, 'That consultation was very impressive, but there is just one more thing I'd like to know. Do you think you could ask your guide if they play sport on the other side?'

The medium scratched her head and said, 'Well now, that's one question I've never asked and I don't know the answer. But come back next week and I'll try to find out for you.'

The following week the man returned and the medium said, 'I've got what you might call some good news and some bad news.'

The man replied: 'Oh, give me the good news first. Tell me, do they have sport on the other side?'

The medium said, 'Yes, they do.'

'Do they play cricket?'

'Yes.'

'Well that's marvellous, fantastic. But what's the bad news?' asked the man.

The medium paused and then said, 'I'm afraid you're captain on Sunday!'

If only those people outside the hall had bothered to step inside, they could have shared the joke with us. They could also have shared the tremendous sense of joy that came with every message from the spirit world, and the comfort those messages brought.

Little Stephen now has a very special place in our flat, with my other spirit children, as do two youngsters who paid a visit while I was doing a demonstration at the Forum Theatre, Manchester.

Again the theatre, which is in the suburb of Wythenshawe, on the outskirts of Manchester, was packed to capacity. I had barely started the demonstration when I noticed a young girl aged about twelve standing in the wings. At first I thought she might be the daughter of someone in the audience who had accidentally strayed on to the stage. She looked so real. But then I realized that nobody, apart from myself, had seen her. She was obviously from the spirit world.

Normally I only hear voices, and only rarely do I see spirits and they're almost always children. Like this young girl they are so real to me that I can mistake them for the flesh and blood youngsters who live here on the earth plane.

I said nothing when I first saw this young girl. She was wearing a sweater and jeans and her long black hair fell down over her shoulders. She seemed hesitant and shy and I realized that this was probably her first attempt at communicating from the spirit world.

'Hello, Doris,' she said. 'I've brought my little cousin along. Would you like to see him?'

This rather took me aback and I didn't say anything to the audience but just nodded to her. She skipped off beaming a great big smile and returned a few seconds later with a gorgeous little boy, about two years old. He was sucking his thumb and dragging a teddy along behind him. It was a lovely sight and I couldn't contain myself any longer.

'I've got a little girl here called Kate and she's with a lovely little boy. They want to say hello to somebody called Rose.' Then turning to the little girl I said, 'Come on, luv, tell us what you want to say?'

She replied, 'Just tell them I'm sorry, Doris. Don't blame my cousin. It was my fault. Mum warned us not to go on the lines, but we did.'

The words were tumbling out as if she was relieved at last to be able to explain what happened. 'You see there was a hole in the fence. We climbed through and then my cousin fell over and I went back to help him. That's when it happened.'

Throughout this conversation the little lad stood studiously sucking his thumb, clutching his teddy and looking up at Kate. Then he took his thumb out of his mouth and spoke for the first time. He had a distinct lisp and said in a surprisingly husky voice, 'Yeth, but tell everybody we're all right now.'

I relayed the message to the audience. It was all so vivid, I described the children, the voices, and said, 'They're here now with us on stage!'

From the back of the theatre I heard a voice shout, 'Dear God they belong to us.'

It was a woman in her mid-fifties. She made her way down the aisle and, as she walked up to the stage and stood in front of me, the little boy jumped up and down shouting, 'Ith our Gran, ith our Gran!'

As I described what was happening, the woman burst into tears and said, 'It's true, Doris. You've got my grandchildren with you. We lost them last year on holiday. Kate's Mum warned them not to go near the railway lines but they did. It was terrible. They were both hit by a train and died instantly.'

I reminded her as gently as I could that they were not dead. They had left the earth plane but now they were in the spirit world. They had come along this evening to prove that in their new life they were quite happy and well cared for. It was all very emotional, and by the end of the contact I don't think there was a dry eye in the theatre.

There was quite a bit of weeping on this tour but I'm happy to say that mostly with joy and laughter! That's the atmosphere I really love, and one of the evenings I remember best was in Derby when an old dear called Nellie had them rolling in the aisles. She really raised the roof.

When her voice first came through I found myself pointing to somewhere around the sixth row of the stalls. I said, 'I want to be somewhere around there and I've got Nellie for someone. I know it's somewhere along either the fifth or sixth row.'

In the sixth row a young woman's voice chirped up, 'Doris, our Mum was called Nellie and she's over on the other side.'

'Well she's popped back to say hello to you,' I replied. 'And I'll tell you something else, one of the people with you was in two minds as to whether or not to come along tonight.'

Without stopping to think, and with Nellie prompting me, I added, 'In fact, she didn't really want to come because she thought I was a bit peculiar.'

Nellie's daughter, whom I later discovered was called Margaret Payton and who lives in Etwall near Derby, spun round to her companion and said, 'Well, I never, you didn't say anything like that to me!'

I butted in, 'No, she didn't, but Nellie's telling me all about it.'

Margaret's friend squirmed a bit in the limelight and I felt a bit sorry because I could see her blushing, so I added, 'Now you're here, luv, it isn't as bad as you thought, is it? I mean we're not scaring anybody or being too serious are we?'

'It's not nearly as bad as I thought,' she laughed.

Then I turned back to Margaret and said, 'Your Mum keeps calling me "me duck".' The effect on her was electrifying. She gasped and said, 'You're right, Doris, she must be with you. That's what she used to call everybody.'

I continued, 'She's just said "Me daughter's just bought herself a new washing-machine, me duck, just you ask her about that!" '

Margaret interrupted and said, 'No, Doris, not a washing-machine. It was a dish-washer.'

Before I had time to think, I then blurted out Nellie's reply word for word. 'She's saying, "Whatever it was, she couldn't get the bloody thing into the kitchen. It wouldn't go through the door!" '

Margaret nearly collapsed and so did the rest of the audience. 'You're right, Doris, you're right.' she shrieked again, almost choking with laughter.

The rest of the theatre was in uproar at this last remark, but now Nellie was in full flight and said, 'That's typical of my girls, buy things first and think afterwards. Wouldn't bloody well fit! I stood there and watched them struggling. I had a right old laugh to myself.'

The audience were hooting with laughter and just to convince everyone she was there I added, 'Nellie's just told me that life was hard for her. You girls are having it much easier, but she's glad to see you have picked up some of her habits.'

Nellie was really enjoying herself. She told me knowingly, 'You see, Doris, me duck, she had an electricity bill which she knew was far too much. She took it back and they knocked fifty-two quid off it. Eee, I were proud about that.'

At this stage the rest of the audience were still

85

giggling over Nellie's earlier outburst and hadn't quite heard the last remark properly. But again Margaret looked as if she'd been given a giant electric shock when I relayed the message. Her jaw dropped in amazement and she said, 'Our Mam always knew everything. But you tell her it wasn't fifty-two pounds we got back. It was only thirty-two! Even so it was very welcome.'

Nellie still hadn't finished having her bit of fun and dutifully I reported the next bit of information she whispered in my ear, I said, 'Margaret, you know that bit of dining-room carpet, the blue bit? Well, it's got a bit rubbed, it's started to wear so you've turned it round. And your Mam's just told me, "The trouble is, Doris, she got it cheap you know. Shouldn't have bought it, of course." '

Again Margaret was astounded by the accuracy and the interest her mother was obviously taking in her family's life down here. And just to make sure everyone knew she was still taking a very active interest, Nellie whispered to me, 'Tell our Margaret I've been to Number 67.'

I asked Margaret, 'Who lives at number 67?'

'My sister,' she replied.

'Well, Nellie's keeping an eye on her as well. She says to tell you she's just been to Number 67! And just to prove it, she says she likes the new gas fire they've just bought.'

That was Nellie's final little triumphant-statement before she left. Her last words were: 'Just tell the family, me duck, I think it's smashing over here, it's lovely, but I'll still keep me eye on them all. I love them just as much as ever.' With that the old girl was gone. But what a character, somebody I'll never forget. And I felt really privileged to have been the one to relay her messages. I looked at Margaret, her eyes were glistening with tears. But they were tears of laughter and all round the hall there was a wonderful happy atmosphere, almost like a carnival. It was one of the funniest demonstrations of the tour. Normally when I've finished a demonstration I feel weak and drained. My stomach and solar plexus ache with the tension of it all. This night I was aching alright, but I honestly thought that I'd split my sides laughing!

Not every chat with the spirit world turns into that sort of cabaret act, of course. Many times the atmosphere is tinged with sadness or regret, because usually after a loved one has passed over, we can think of so many things we should have said to them when they were with us in body. Or, we can think of so many other things we should not have said. Whatever the case, there's no need to spend time brooding over it. Your loved ones are still as close as they ever were. They know how you're feeling. And they understand.

If only those of us on the earth plane took more time to try to understand each other we'd have a lot less rows. A little patience and tolerance go a long way to making the world a better place to live in. Mind you, I have to admit like anybody else there are times when my own patience is stretched to breaking point. Like when we were at Stoke-on-Trent. It wasn't the religious hecklers singing their hymns at the top of their voices all evening that bothered me. It was the flock of starlings which decided to give me a dawn chorus – all night long!

John and I had been booked into a lovely old hotel opposite the station. It was like all the old-fashioned railway hotels with high ceilings and nice deep carpets. We had a nice room, too, looking out on to a cluster of trees. The problem was that this was also the home of millions of starlings. Or at least it seemed like millions. During the day it was nice and restful, but as dusk descended so did the starlings. The air was almost black with them. It was incredible and the first time I saw this phenomena I shouted to John. 'There must be an awful thunderstorm brewing up. The sky's suddenly gone very dark.' But of course it wasn't clouds that had blotted out the light. It was this huge flock of birds.

They had settled on the tree outside our bedroom window which was on the first floor. It was an unbelievable sight. Every single branch was smothered in birds. There wasn't a leaf or a branch to be seen.

The hall porter told me he was as puzzled as we were: 'I've never seen anything like it either, Mrs Stokes,' he said with a twinkle in his eye. 'Looks as if every starling in the Potteries has turned out to welcome you!'

I just gazed at this massive flock in awe. The noise they were making was almost deafening. As we left for the demonstration at Hanley I remember thinking, 'isn't nature fascinating?'

It wasn't quite so fascinating however, when we returned at midnight. The starlings were still there. And still chirping away, although by now the noise they were making was definitely not music to my ears. Both John and I spent the entire night with the window tightly shut, the curtains drawn and pillows over our heads. But even this didn't completely drown the noise. It vanished, along with the birds, round about dawn. And again throughout the day it was blissfully quiet in our room.

Then, just as the sun began to fade, the starlings reappeared by the thousand and started singing again. I groaned to John, 'I can't stand much more of this, luv.

I'll go crackers if we have another night like last night. Nature's lovely and it's nice to see birds happy, but you can have too much of a good thing.' And to my amazement when John and I returned to the hotel again at midnight I felt something very strange had happened. At first I couldn't place it and then I suddenly clutched John's arm and said, 'It's the starlings, they've gone!' They had. There wasn't a tweet to be heard. It was most puzzling.

Then the night porter spotted me and strode over to tell us, 'It was quite extraordinary, Mrs Stokes. There were more starlings than ever in that tree outside your bedroom tonight. In fact it was too much for the poor old tree, a branch snapped and came crashing down. It startled the birds so much they flew away and haven't come back.'

I went out on to the hotel forecourt. The branch that had snapped was at least six inches thick. No matter how rotten it had been, it surely couldn't have been brought down by the weight of a flock of birds.

A friend suggested that the spirit world had given me some assistance, I couldn't believe that my friends in the spirit world would turn their hand to bird scaring. At least I hoped not, because when that branch came crashing down it had made a very severe dent in the roof of a very smart car parked beneath it! I can only say that both John and I slept very soundly in our beds that night and didn't bother to delve into the mystery too deeply.

Chapter Nine

Our trip to Brighton was a sort of double celebration for me. Three weeks earlier I had thought I might have to cancel the appearance yet again when I was called back to hospital for more tests. I'd been getting nagging pains under my right shoulder for more than a month. At first I'd shrugged it off and put that awful doubt, which even now I get occasionally, to the back of my mind. But eventually the pain became sharper and even John's healing touch wasn't enough. I had to go to the doctor who ordered me into hospital.

I wouldn't say that the Charing Cross hospital is exactly home from home, but I've been in and out of it so many times I've come to regard it as more or less my second home! And the wonderful the nursing staff do their best to cushion the blow whenever I'm admitted and their cheerfulness certainly helps to make it bearable. But, as so many of you will know, no matter how much the staff may try to cheer you up there comes a time when you feel desperately alone with nothing but your own thoughts. And they can be terrifying.

The moment of truth came for me on the first night, after John had kissed me good night and gone back home to cook his supper! The lights in the ward had been dimmed and silence had settled over the whole building. Even the sound of the London traffic had died away to nothing more than a murmur in the distance. Suddenly, I felt lonely and a bit frightened. As I lay there in surroundings which had by now become all too familiar to me – I've been in and out of hospital for the past four years – I faced up to the question that I'd been pushing to the back of my mind for weeks. I said a little prayer out loud, 'Please God, if it is cancer again, don't let me linger. Take me quickly.'

I said that prayer in a half-world hovering between consciousness and sleep – but somebody was listening. A voice I recognized instantly as Ramonov's came to me, cutting sharply through the mist of semi-consciousness, saying gently but firmly, 'Rest child, you still have much work to do.' Without realizing the implications, I drifted off into a sound sleep.

For three days I was prodded and pinched and examined and peered at, and taken up and down in the lift for x-rays so many times I felt like a yoyo. At the end of that time the only thing they could tell me with certainty was that there was no sign of a recurrence of cancer! I wept with joy and thanked God for this new lease of life and then, on the fourth day, there was an added bonus.

A surgeon who specialized in the nervous system put his finger on the problem. I was suffering from a trapped and damaged nerve below my right shoulder blade. The answer was shock treatment – and that was how I became known as Doris Stokes the bionic medium!

I was given a little black box to carry in my pocket and electrodes were attached to the damaged spot – this way electric shocks were sent through my system. It wasn't quite as bad as it sounds. The shocks, which came every five or ten seconds, just produced a mild tingling sensation, and I thought, 'Well, if it eases the pain, I can put up with wearing this blessed thing for an hour or so.'

I was sitting at the side of my bed when the surgeon came to see how I was getting on. 'Oh it's not too bad,' I said. 'I can manage with it for a couple of hours a day.'

He chuckled and said, 'I've got news for you, Mrs Stokes. You'll be wearing it for eight hours a day. And furthermore, I'd just like to take a quick look at that little box of tricks to make sure it's working properly.'

It wasn't, of course. The electric current was turned down as low as it would go, and when the surgeon adjusted it, it really did give me a shock. But somehow I felt I could survive anything, after all I didn't have cancer, and I knew this shock treatment wasn't going to last for ever. By the second day, I had become used to the voltage and the pain in my shoulder was definitely easing. But the treatment certainly had a peculiar side effect.

I wasn't completely confined to bed, but I wasn't allowed to dress so I wandered around the ward in an orange nylon nightie. It was on the third day, when I was back at home, with my box of tricks that the strangest thing happened.

One morning I'd got up out of bed to make a cup of tea, and as I reached out to open the kitchen door I heard an extremely loud crackling sound. It could only have lasted for a second or so, but I glanced at myself in the mirror in the hall. It was one of the funniest things I've ever seen: me and my orange nightie were surrounded by a bright orange glow.

It had obviously been caused by some sort of build-up of static electricity, but it looked almost supernatural – and very comical. I walked back into the bedroom a few minutes later with a cup of tea for John still chuckling to myself.

'What's so funny, then?' he asked.

'You should have been here a while back and you'd have seen it for yourself,' I replied: 'You know, I think I must be the only medium in the world who's been able to get a glimpse of her own aura – it was hilarious!'

It was in this mood that John and I arrived in Brighton and booked into a seafront hotel. It was still only early March but that day on the South Coast was one of glorious sunshine, the first real day of spring. It was so warm that we opened the french windows overlooking a sea that was as blue as those I could remember from my childhood. And on that day I felt as carefree as ever I had been as a youngster!

I've never been to India but, as far as I'm concerned, the Taj Mahal couldn't be any more beautiful than the Royal Pavilion in Brighton. It looks gorgeous with its many domes glistening in the sunlight. Just behind the Pavilion, which was built by a Prince who had more money than sense, is the dome that was once the royal riding stables. Now it's been converted into a beautiful theatre which holds two thousand people, and on the night that John and I visited it every seat had been taken and the atmosphere was fantastic.

It was almost three months to the day that I had been forced to cancel the original demonstration there and I could see now why I had received so many flowers from wellwishers in the area. The audience really was marvellous, warm and welcoming. And, once again, there was a fair number of young people among them. As I went in through the back door of the theatre, I was stopped by a couple of young lads, teenagers, and one of them said, 'It is Doris, isn't it? We've been waiting here for more than an hour. Could you please do something for us?'

I didn't know what to say. I certainly didn't want to have a sitting here on the pavement. But I needn't have worried. The elder of the two simply said, 'Please, Doris, could we have your autograph?'

I was lost for words. It was so touching that at first I didn't know what to say but signed with a flourish. It just goes to show that it isn't only old dears like me that are interested in spiritualism, more and more young people are getting involved.

The atmosphere inside the Dome was one of excitement and expectancy. You could almost see it in the air and there was a continual buzz of conversation as the audience poured in. Backstage I was doing my best to relax, but as usual my tummy was turning somersaults. I suppose really it's because, I never know what sort of messages are going to come through, or even if the spirit world is going to let me down altogether, that I feel apprehensive.

Certainly on this evening I wasn't prepared for the first couple of visitors. We had begun with some preliminary chit-chat and I'd just explained about the young lads wanting my autograph, when a voice in my ear said, 'I'm Edie, Doris, and I'd like to say hello to the twins. It's their birthday on February 17th.' I duly relayed the message, which was recognized by a lady sitting in the stalls.

'That's my Mum, Doris, we've got twins in the family,' she called out. 'The birthday is in fact February 7th not 17th. You must have misheard that bit.'

Suddenly I heard a cat mewing and Edie said, 'Tell them I've brought Lucky along with me!'

I said, 'Did Mum have a cat called Lucky?'

'Good gracious, yes!' came the reply.

'Well,' I said, 'we've got Lucky here too. He's come

along to show that animals can live on just as well in the spirit world.'

At this a giggle went round the theatre, and then Edie said, 'They've just had the house pebble-dashed.'

I said out loud, 'That sounds very peculiar, what an odd thing to say, but Edie tells me you've had your house pebble-dashed.'

There was more astonishment in the voice this time as the young lady replied, 'Well actually, Doris, it was snowcemed.'

As quick as a flash, Edie replied, 'They can use whatever fancy name they like. I say it's been pebble-dashed!'

When I relayed this information there was a roar of laughter from all over the theatre. It might have been a trivial message to some people's ears, but Edie was simply letting her own folk know that although she had passed over, both she and Lucky the cat were still keeping a friendly eye on the family – even if they didn't know the difference between pebble-dash and snowcem!

The second contact of the evening also produced some laughter, but I felt uneasy. There was also an undercurrent of sadness, some personal tragedy which I could sense but not pinpoint accurately and it wasn't until after the demonstration that the full story was revealed.

Up in the balcony I could see a strong blue light glowing steadily. To me it indicated a spirit that had been over for some time, quite settled in the other world, but now wanting to pass on a message to someone in this audience. The name 'Jackson' came through to me and, sure enough, beneath that blue light sat a lady who later told me her full name was Elizabeth Jackson.

I said, 'I can't see you up there properly, luv, and I hate talking to a blob in the distance. Come downstairs and let's have a chat.'

As Mrs Jackson made her way down to the front of the auditorium a woman's voice in my ear said: 'I had the same problem as you, Doris, but I wasn't so lucky.'

I knew what she meant so I asked her outright: 'You mean you had your boob off, luv.'

'Yes,' she replied. And then she gave me the name 'Ada'. By this time Mrs Jackson was standing in front of me. She was an attractive, dark haired and smartly dressed lady but she seemed to have such sad eyes.

I said, 'Did your mum have a mastectomy?'

Those eyes transformed as if by magic. They lit up like a couple of twinkling stars. 'Yes, Doris, she did.'

'Was her name Ada?'

Even bigger twinkling stars now as her face broke into a broad grin and she said, 'Yes, that's right!'

There was no stopping Ada now she had got through to her daughter. It was several years since she had passed over but this was the first time she had communicated with Elizabeth.

I dutifully relayed the messages as they came through and Elizabeth verified them as we went along. Ada said, 'I'm back in perfect health now, just as I used to be, as young as ever. I had a right old time with that cancer, but now its all behind me and I want Elizabeth to remember me as I was before I became ill.'

The she mentioned a brown teapot and I said to Elizabeth, 'Mum's talking about a brown teapot. She used to keep money in it . . .'

Elizabeth interrupted, laughing, 'She used to throw it at my Dad when he took the money out.'

The audience were loving it and roared with laughter but suddenly I sensed a change in the atmosphere. In front of me was a sea of smiling faces, but Ada's voice had become serious. She whispered in my ear, 'There's going to a parting. Tell her to get everything sorted out and see a solicitor.'

It was a strange sort of message and had there just been Elizabeth and myself I would have told her. But it didn't seem the thing to do in front of two hundred people. I had to be tactful. A message had been given and it was my duty to relay it, but to do so without causing any embarrassment.

I said to her, 'Your Mum says she sends her love. She asks that you be happy and I should add that I know there are some problems but I can't go into details. Go and see a solicitor.'

Elizabeth looked at me knowingly, and said, 'I will. Thank you, Doris. You've been a great help.'

It was only later that evening that Elizabeth, who's home is in Brighton, revealed exactly what that message meant to her. She talked to a journalist who had been covering the demonstration and later gave me permission to make it public.

'The accuracy of Doris's statements astonished me. I have never had any communication with her whatsoever before this evening, but she was absolutely right about everything she mentioned.

'I nearly fainted when she talked about that teapot. Even the colour was right and it was something that we had never mentioned outside the family. It proved to me that there is an afterlife and that my mother was there with me in this theatre tonight.

'I've been to see quite a few mediums recently. I've been desperately looking for some sort of reassurance that there is an afterlife, but until this evening I've searched in vain. That's all changed now, I've got the evidence I was looking for, all the proof I need, and I can face what's in store for me knowing that at the end of it all I'll be reunited with the people I love.'

Elizabeth was speaking calmly and, as the journalist told me later, there was no warning of the bombshell she dropped with her last remark.

'Doris, in fact, was uncannily accurate about my own problems, and I'll take Mum's advice about seeing a solicitor and getting everything sorted out. Until tonight I hadn't the heart to do anything. It all seemed so pointless because I'd received no proof but, as I said, all that's changed. You see, I'm suffering from an incurable illness. I've only got a few months left but I feel now as if I'm almost looking forward to passing over.'

The story of Elizabeth begs the question: Why is it some of us have to suffer so much? That evening in Brighton, just a few minutes after I had been speaking to Elizabeth, another young woman asked, 'Why do some children have to suffer so dreadfully, Doris?'

It was evident from her own sad face that she had lost a child of her own, and my heart went out to her immediately. To lose a mother or father, sister or brother is hard. But for a mother to lose her child is indescribable. It's part of you that dies and never comes to life again on this earth plane. The anguish is something that only another mother in a similar position can possibly hope to understand, which is why with this young mother I felt that affinity.

I could only tell her what I firmly believe: and that is

that those who spend only a short time here are God's specially chosen ones, they don't need to spend such a long time on the earth plane.

Another questioner at Brighton asked me, 'Will I have to meet up with my step-mother again? She was cruel to me both mentally and physically before she passed over and, honestly Doris, I couldn't bear to have to speak to her.'

I always feel very sad when I hear remarks like this and particularly, as in this case, when it wasn't coming from a youngster. I told her, 'Please try not to feel bitter, it doesn't help. If your step-mother was such a demon to you, there's no chance of you bumping into her on the other side.

'She'll be on her way back down here to start the long climb up that ladder again, but you ought to try to find it in your heart to wish her well because she's going to need all the help she can get.

'Have a word with your spirit guide tonight and say, "Help me to get rid of this bitterness I feel because it's spoiling my life".'

But there were, of course, lots of vivid and happy memories and I don't think anyone in the theatre will ever forget little Lainee. Ten years old, big blue eyes and fair hair, she danced on the stage for ten minutes. Only a tiny flickering blue light overhead, which faded away to almost nothing on occasions, indicated she was a spirit child who had passed over very recently.

In front of her stood her Auntie Leslie who confirmed that in fact Lainee had passed over just three days before.

Her mother's grief was understandable and she had been too upset to face coming to the theatre. Auntie Leslie, who was in fact her closest friend, had come along on the merest off chance that there might be some comfort to be drawn. She never in her life expected to be able to contact the child herself. In fact I could see there was still doubt in her eyes as I described Lainee.

But then the little girl said cheekily, 'Tell Auntie Leslie that I know my brother David's now got my watch. He's wearing it and I think it suits him.'

With that she gave a great big grin, and I could see one of her front teeth was chipped. At this bit of information Auntie Leslie dissolved into tears.

And then, twirling the curls of her fringe round her little finger, Lainee said, 'Thank you for letting me come. I wanted to because Mummy is so sad but please tell Auntie Leslie to make sure Mummy knows I haven't really gone away.'

And then, as a parting message to reassure everybody she really was with us, Lainee said, 'And make sure you give all my love to Michelle.'

This was her closest friend who had been with her shortly before she died of leukaemia.

It had been a very emotional evening and later Mike Kiddey told me he had seen a theatre usherette sobbing her heart out by the stage door.

There were tears streaming down her face as she blurted out: 'Oh doesn't Doris bring such a lot of comfort!'

I thought, I'm not quite sure how to take that! But on the other hand a good cry always does you a power of good, doesn't it?

Chapter Ten

1984 began for me with a little chat to George Orwell. Well it wasn't so much a cosy little talk, rather more a lecture by George with me sitting and listening all meek and mild. And it was hardly an intimate occasion either. The whole episode was recorded and shown to millions of television viewers on the West coast of America.

It was an experience that I shall never forget. And I know the television crew won't either. Mr Orwell got very annoyed and at one stage threatened to sabotage the filming!

His real name was Eric Arthur Blair and he died over thirty years ago. Most people know of him as the author of 1984, in which he predicted that our lives would be ruled by Big Brother. I'd heard about the book, of course, but I'd never read it. Books like that are not my cup of tea. I believe there are enough problems as it is, without imagining more or reading about things that could happen. But as 1984 approached all the papers were getting worked up about it and stories on the subject were appearing almost daily. I wasn't particularly interested since Christmas was approaching and I was much more involved in preparing for this wonderful time of year.

I love the spirit of Christmas – it's especially wonderful for the little ones – and am always sad when the festivities are over. If only we could sustain all that love and harmony throughout the year . . . So for me a far bigger problem than George Orwell and 1984 was where to hang all the Christmas cards that were cascading through our letter box. There were so many of them.

By Christmas Eve there was hardly a piece of wallpaper which wasn't covered with nativity scenes, robins, snowmen or bells and the mantelpiece had completely disappeared under a virtual blizzard of cards! It gave John and I a nice warm feeling to think that beyond our own four walls we had hundreds of unseen friends who had taken the trouble to wish us a happy Christmas. Thank you all so very much.

I was pinning the latest cards to the wall when the telephone rang.

A voice said, 'Hi there, Mrs Stokes, what are you doing on New Year's Eve?'

It was a bouncy, enthusiastic voice and not one I recognised. I knew quite well what I would be doing on New Year's Eve. I'd watch the telly with John and, more likely than not, be tucked up in bed long before they rang the New Year in. But I said, 'I'm not sure what we're doing. Why do you want to know?'

'Well,' said the voice. 'We'd like you to talk to George Orwell for us.'

I didn't know what to say! I'd had some funny requests in my time, but this one beat the lot. I was so flabbergasted I replied without thinking, 'Oh I see, all right then.'

'Great stuff,' the caller enthused. I could almost see him bouncing up and down with pleasure. 'We'll be in touch.'

Then I managed to collect my thoughts and said, 'Hold on, I forgot to ask who you were!'

It transpired a film would be made for a Los Angeles television company, as part of a series on psychic phenomena from around the world.

I chuckled to myself because I had visions of this big American tv producer, puffing on his cigar, shouting, 'I got this great idea. We're gonna get someone to talk to George Orwell in the Noo Year.' I still don't know to this day how they came up with my name, but the caller said, 'I knew we could rely on your help, Doris. We'll be round to see you as soon as possible to discuss the details.'

I replied, 'Don't rush. At least let us have Christmas Dinner first!'

A few minutes later John came home from the shops. I heard him open the door while I was in the kitchen, and I shouted to him, 'I've got a little surprise for you. We're going out on New Year's Eve.'

'That'll make a nice change,' he said.

'Yes, and guess who I'm going to be talking to?'

'I've no idea, luv.'

I paused for a second and then said: 'George Orwell.'

'Well, I never,' replied my husband. But after being together for so many years, absolutely nothing comes as a surprise to John. He takes it all in his stride.

The comings and goings at our flat have been accepted as completely normal by the neighbours, so nobody batted an eyelid when tv cameras turned up a couple of days before New Year's Eve. My friend Nancy had just popped in for a cup of tea when the technicians arrived.

'We'll forget the tea,' she said. 'I'll get out of the way.'

'You'll do no such thing,' I retorted crossly. 'Stay put and watch the fun. I've no idea what they want me to do and it might be a bit of a hoot.'

And that was how Nancy, war-widow and fellow spiritualist, found herself in a new role for the afternoon. She became a television interviewer!

As the technicians unwound miles of cables round

the flat, the chief cameraman told me what he wanted me to do.

'It's easy, Doris. Just speak straight into the camera. Tell us all about yourself, why you became a medium and the experiences you've had, the mystery that surrounds it all, and any miracles you can think of off hand.'

'Hold on,' I replied. 'There's no mysteries or miracles. It's the most natural thing in the world and, anyway, what's this got to do with George Orwell?'

'We've got to get some atmosphere, background and the rest. We'll be doing the actual scene when you contact George Orwell in Ipswich.'

I thought to myself, 'They're taking a lot for granted. I don't know yet whether or not George wants to talk to us and, if he doesn't, no amount of rushing or dashing about by cameramen is going to make him.' But I kept that thought to myself and simply said, 'Fine, but I can't just stand here looking at a camera and talking about myself. I feel daft! You'll have to get someone to interview me and ask questions.'

The cameraman replied, 'That'll mean cancelling today's shooting, Doris, until we can get somebody here.'

I looked at all the equipment scattered round the parlour and the kitchen and thought, 'I can't have all this mess again.' Then I had a brainwave. 'How about Nancy,' I cried.

Nancy nearly dropped her cup and saucer with surprise. But she agreed and it worked a treat. We just sat casually in our parlour while Nancy asked me about spiritualism. Of course, she knows all about it as well so she's used to the sort of questions we get asked, but the film crew found it intriguing. In fact, I could tell when they first arrived that they were a bit sceptical

104

about mediumship. But after the filming the head cameraman said to me, 'That was terrific. So natural and sincere. It was a stroke of genius to choose Nancy to help.'

The film crew couldn't wait to get to Ipswich. As for myself, I wasn't so sure. I hadn't read anything about the man or the book but I had a distinctly uneasy feeling that Mr Orwell might prove to be difficult. How right I was, as I discovered a couple of nights later.

The first disappointment came with a phone call the next day. We wouldn't be spending New Year's Eve in Ipswich. The hotel into which we had been booked, and where we were to do the filming, was, naturally enough, holding a New Year's Eve dance. The film director felt that the noise might not be conducive to a demonstration of mediumship. From the feeling I was getting about Mr Orwell I concluded he definitely wouldn't want to make contact in a place full of people wearing funny hats and having a party. He just didn't seem to be that type of man.

It was agreed that John and I would travel down to Ipswich on New Year's Day, so we did spend New Year's Eve watching the telly.

But that night I just couldn't get to sleep for worrying about the next morning's filming, so I thought, 'Why not try to contact him now?' Normally, of course, when I make contact with the spirit world and pass on messages, I am doing it on behalf of somebody who is with me at the time. I act as the bridge that links the two sides. Not that night, however. There was just me, and hopefully George.

I concentrated very hard and said to myself, 'Come on, George. I don't know anything about you, and yet I'm supposed to be trying to contact you in the morning. Please have a chat with me now, just to give me some background information so that we don't link up as complete strangers.'

Very briefly with my third eye I saw a face. It seemed sunken and haggard with dark hair. But the most vivid impression was that of a scar on the neck. Then a posh, strong but impatient voice came through, saying, 'Who are you, woman? I don't know you, what do you want?'

'Good lord, it's George!' I heard myself saying.

Having made the contact, I decided to ignore his rather abrupt manner and asked, 'I've not read your book, but is 1984 anything like you predicted it would be?'

He replied in a distinct Lancashire accent, 'I'll tell you now, luv, in many ways it's a damn sight worse!'

I couldn't work out this abrupt change in accents. That plum in the mouth had completely disappeared and the voice was warmer, even kindly. It might have been another spirit talking but I knew it wasn't. It was still Orwell, of that I was convinced, and later I was told he had indeed spent much of his life in Lancashire.

Orwell again switched back to his upper class accent and said, 'Listen to me, woman. This world will certainly destroy itself. Or rather, you mortals will destroy both this wonderful earth and each other unless you do something about it. That's what I kept trying to tell people.' He was getting very angry, I could tell.

I said, 'Well, where's the Big Brother you were on about who was going to watch over us and rule our lives?'

'Look around you, woman.' There was a sneer in his voice.

'Why do you take such a dim view of the world?' I

asked. 'I shouldn't think you made many friends. You'd have been too glum.'

I could almost hear him sighing as he added, 'I didn't have many friends. I wasn't accepted by my own class of people. They couldn't understand me. And the working classes wouldn't accept me either, although I tried to mingle with them. All my life I was searching for an identity I never found.'

There was silence for a few seconds, then a chuckle, and the voice switched back yet again into broad Lancashire: 'Enough of this, lass! Sort your own problems out on earth before yer start asking about mine.'

I replied, 'It's by learning from other people's mistakes as well as our own that we can make this world a better place. And it's no skin off your nose to offer a bit of advice.'

The voice became petulant and upper-crust again. It snapped: 'I do not like the human race. I do not like its silly face.' And then he was gone. Abruptly and without warning.

I tried like mad to contact him again, concentrating so hard that it gave me a headache. But it was no use. In the distance I heard a clock chime. It was two o'clock in the morning on January 1st 1984. I thought to myself, 'Thank you for coming through, Mr Orwell. But you might at least have wished me a Happy New Year before you vanished again!' He was definitely not a happy soul. Before I dropped off into that deep sleep that always follows a contact with the spirit world, I said a prayer. I prayed that 1984 might bring a little more peace and understanding here on earth and a little less bitterness in the soul of George Orwell.

The Great White Horse is a beautiful hotel standing

near the centre of Ipswich. It dates back hundreds of years and as soon as I walked in I felt at home. It was restful, steeped in history and had plenty of atmosphere. The staff tell you proudly that Lord Nelson stayed there, as did Charles Dickens – the inn played an important part in the life of Samuel Pickwick in *The Pickwick Papers*. What the guide books don't tell you is that George Orwell had also slept there on more than one occasion. Nor do they reveal that it was at the Great White Horse he lost his temper. But he did, and it happened while we were filming there for the American tv programme.

The company had chosen Ipswich because this was where Orwell, or rather Eric Arthur Blair, had spent quite some time. He had taken his pen name from the River Orwell that runs through the town, and I suppose the tv film makers thought it might be easier for me to make contact with the man in surroundings that were familiar to him. It does help a little, but it is far more important to have someone who knew him in his lifetime and someone with whom he might want to talk. And that goes for any contact in the spirit world. I can't demand anything of them, I can only ask. And they are more likely to respond to requests when a loved one is by my side. On this occasion, we didn't have anyone who knew Orwell personally, but quite a few experts and a load of text books to check any facts that I might unearth during the course of the sitting.

A rickety old taxi had called for us at 10 a.m. to take us to Ipswich and looking back on it, it was an hilarious ride: the driver lost his way and since his car had almost no springs, we felt as if we were sitting on the floor, with our noses barely reaching the windows. By the time John, Nancy and myself got to Ipswich they almost had to prise us out of the taxi with a tin opener. We were so stiff we could barely walk!

So, naturally, the first thing we wanted on arrival was a cup of tea. As we sat in the covered courtyard, which had been turned into a very comfortable lounge, the television director explained exactly what he planned to do.

There would be a panel of eight people, of all ages and backgrounds, who had some knowledge of Orwell plus others sitting in the wings with the text books. The cameras would roll and somehow I was to produce George Orwell out of a hat, or rather thin air. Actually I don't think the television people knew what to expect at all. I heard the director ask someone as I arrived: 'What happens? Does she go into a trance or something? I mean, what are we going to *see*?'

I explained, as gently as I could, that he wasn't going to be filming a television spectacular with choirs of angels or ghosts walking through walls. 'It's just Doris talking that you'll hear, luv, and if George wants to talk to me all well and good. If he doesn't, there's not much I can do about it.'

I could see he looked a bit disappointed, so to cheer him up a bit I added, 'I have already spoken to him.'

The director's face lost its worried look – until I added, 'And I can tell you now he can be an awkward old so and so!'

Tea break over, we all filed into the lounge where the camera, lights and sound equipment had been set up. Chairs had been arranged in a semi-circle with all the microphones trained on them. The arc lights were so strong it was impossible to look directly at them, and the heat they emitted was enough to melt the ice on the pavements outside. I knew immediately this was not going to be an easy sitting.

109

John was with me which was a comfort. He always sits in the wings when I do demonstrations in theatres but this was different. That air of excitement was there all right. But there was no warmth flooding up from an audience. Just a cold impersonal camera and those lights, which were enough to roast you. There were no families eagerly hoping to contact loved ones who had passed over. At first I couldn't put my finger on what was really wrong with the atmosphere. Then it struck me: there was no love in the air.

The director sat me down and put a glass of water by my side. Everybody else took their seats around me. There was a shout of 'Lights' and for a second or two I was dazzled. I cleared my throat and began talking as calmly as I possibly could.

'Now you all know why we are here. We're going to try and get through to George Orwell. I must tell you now that I have managed to tune into him and he seems to be a very difficult man indeed.'

As I spoke, I was straining frantically for the smallest whisper of a voice in my ear. Nothing came through but I could sense the agitation around me.

I ploughed on, turning to a young man called James over on my left. 'What was it you wanted to ask George Orwell?'

James wanted to know what Orwell's view of 1984 would have been had he known there was going to be such a proliferation of nuclear weapons.

Still not a whisper, and quite honestly I can't say I wasn't thankful. The last thing I could cope with would be some deep, intellectual discussion about nuclear weapons. That sort of argument is on a much higher plane than I am.

Another questioner butted in, 'Why did he have such a depressed view of life?'

Then it happened. The voice I'd heard only a few hours earlier, haughty and petulant, snapped back, 'I do not like the human race. I do not like its silly face!' There was silence again. I said aloud, 'Oh for goodness' sake, don't go away again, George. We've got to talk to you.'

The voice replied, 'Listen, woman. I've told you I don't know you. Who are you? Have you met Richard?' We were starting to get somewhere, and I shouted out, full of excitement, 'We've got him! He's coming through.'

But before I could say anything else, the director shouted, 'O.K., fine. Hold it!' Then he turned to me, and said, 'Now, I don't know the procedure on these matters, but what I would like to do is . . .'

What he would like to do! I couldn't believe it. Was I supposed to hold some spirit in suspended animation while they adjusted the angle of the camera or dabbed a bit more make-up on someone?

It was my turn to interrupt, 'I can't stop,' I said. 'Hold on, come back, George, or should I call you Eric?'

'I am George Orwell.' It was the haughty voice again, but then, a little more gently he said: 'I tried to take myself over once, you know.'

The heat from the lamps was becoming unbearable and here was Mr Orwell having fun and games at my expense. He was trying to confuse me. I thought, 'Nobody's going to believe what he's doing.' Silently I pleaded, 'George, will you please stop mucking about! Give them some proof you're here.'

That did it. There was an almighty crash as one of the huge arc lights toppled over. It was standing at least three feet from the nearest technician and missed the cameraman by inches. Everybody in that room, including me, must have jumped six inches into the air. It was a miracle nobody was injured. It was even more miraculous that the arc lamp didn't break and that the light didn't go out. We could carry on filming.

'Who the hell tripped over the cables?' yelled the director. There was silence. 'Come on,' he insisted. 'Who was the clumsy-footed so and so?'

The cameraman who answered said quietly, 'I promise you, nobody was within a yard of that lamp or the cables. Nobody was even moving when it happened.' There was another uncomfortable silence. I knew what everybody was thinking, but it was something nobody dared say. So I licked my lips and piped up, 'It's George. He doesn't like to be interrupted when he's passing on a message. You shouldn't have put a stop to it when he came through. That was just a little sign to prove he's here. But don't provoke him any more or Lord alone knows what he'll do next.'

The director looked bewildered. He just said, 'OK, everybody, we'll take a five minute break.' It was more than welcome. I hadn't felt so tense for years. And everybody else around me had thoughtful expressions on their faces. But I had told them. George Orwell could be a very difficult customer when he wanted to be.

We tried again. This time a picture of a bridge over the River Orwell came into my mind. A voice, I couldn't be sure this time it was the author, said it was one of his favourite spots. The faces around me looked puzzled. It meant nothing to them. Then I saw something else: a faint blue light. It was flickering over the girl sitting directly in front of me. This was something I did understand. It meant a spirit was trying to make contact.

I said to the girl, 'Luv, I've got a lady here with a cerebral haemorrhage. She's passed over. I know we're

Here I am with little Daniel Matthews, the baby I named on our visit to Liverpool.

A welcome break in Ipswich where I gave a demonstration to the ducks!

John and I with Bert Weedon who composed and arranged some beautiful music for my long playing record. It brought tears to my eyes.

Waiting for George Orwell in Ipswich. I'm getting my last minute instructions before the cameras roll – and before that arc lamp fell over and the lights dimmed!

A happy moment.

Some of those lovely
smiling faces that make
the long hours worthwhile.

At the Apollo in Coventry I followed stars such as Bucks Fizz and Little and Large. I said they should have billed it as Little and Large plus one large lady!

It was wonderful how many youngsters came to see me on the tour.

Chris Mott, the manager at the Odeon in Birmingham, always made me very welcome. Thank you for looking after me, Chris! Here he is presenting me with a bouquet of flowers at the end of the evening.

It's always hard to say goodbye, even at the end of a demonstration. Nobody wanted me to leave the stage.

Danny La Rue and I at the Odeon, Birmingham. We have remained firm friends – he even popped in at our Ruby Wedding celebrations.

here to contact Orwell, but this is somebody else. They want to pass on a message and I can't ignore it. I know it's for you. She's saying she went to sleep and woke up on the other side.'

The girl gasped. She hadn't expected this. It was George Orwell we were all waiting for. But she said: 'Doris, that's my Mum!'

I said, 'Who's Margaret?'

'My dad's second wife.'

'Your Mum says she's quite happy they're together. It doesn't worry her and she says they get on quite well considering! She also tells me you were upset when your Dad gave Margaret the ring.'

'Yes, Doris, I was.'

'Well don't upset yourself, dear, your Mum doesn't want you to be unhappy. Tell me, who's Doris – apart from me, of course? That's the name I keep getting.'

The girl gasped again, 'That's Mum's name.'

I thought, oh no, we're getting into a sitting we're not supposed to be involved in but I may as well turn it to some advantage. Out loud I said, 'Listen, Doris, luv, can you get that George Orwell to get started? He's the one standing next to you saying nothing.'

Suddenly I experienced a new sensation. I said, 'I feel as if I'm going down a coal mine.'

One of the panel said, 'Orwell lived in a mining village.' He was back again, speaking in that scolding upper crust tone, 'I understand you came to ask me questions. Well do it, woman!'

A young man sitting alongside me said, 'Why did he go to Burma?'

The voice in my ear replied, 'I was looking for the secret of life.'

I had to giggle at that one: 'You certainly went a long way. You could have found it here if you'd looked

113

properly. Surely there was no need to go all the way to Burma.'

'I couldn't have found it here,' he replied. 'I had to find an identity, do something on my own. I was in the police in Burma.'

'That must have been a tough old job then?' I said. We seemed to be getting on a little better now.

He replied, 'It was. You know, woman, I think I must have been a little bit peculiar.'

'Sounds to me as if you were more than just a little bit, luv.' The words were out of my mouth before I'd had time to realize what I was saying. I braced myself for a tirade of abuse, but it never came. Instead Orwell repeated something of what he had said to me during the night, which I relayed to the other people in the room.

'I admit now that I was psychic, although I didn't know it at the time. I didn't know how to handle it. I could see how the future might shape up.

'The only way to get it out of my system was to sit down and write about it as if it were fiction. But times have changed and are not quite as I'd expected. Even so, you must not let yourself be treated just as numbers.'

Then he turned on me again, 'What are you going to do about it, woman?

'I honestly don't know what we're going to do,' I replied. 'I think it's a bit late for me. I'll probably be popping me clogs and joining you soon. It's the youngsters I worry about. They're the ones who have got to sort it out.'

There really was no pleasing the man. I think that remark must have offended him. Either that, or he thought that a working-class woman like Doris Stokes should know better than to try to discuss such things with her betters.

Whatever the reason, Mr Orwell showed his displeasure again. Suddenly the lights went out and we were left in a shadowy gloom with only the sound of the whirring cameras.

'Hold it!' shouted the director again. 'Don't anybody tell me. It's George playing tricks on us. He's determined to make his point, isn't he?' Even more strange, nobody could find a cause for the failure. Or at least they couldn't find an earthly one. It hadn't affected the rest of the hotel, nor the camera which recorded it. It wasn't caused by a blown fuse and moments later the lights worked perfectly again.

But while we had electricity to power the lights once more, the power of the vibrations between myself and Orwell was starting to weaken.

The camera started to roll and two names came through. The voice was still upper class, and it said, 'Lucy's here, but have you seen Richard?' It was the same name he had mentioned to me during the night.

'Who are Lucy and Richard,' I asked the panel. Several people answered almost at once, 'Richard was his adopted son.' Nobody could place Lucy and there was a frantic rustling of paper as the pages of the reference books were turned rapidly. No clues were forthcoming, but somebody said, 'Would Orwell like to live on earth in 1984?'

There was a hollow laugh in my ear. 'No, No. I'm glad I'm out of it, woman. I didn't care much for the earth world when I lived there thirty years ago, I care even less for it now. 1984 isn't as bad as it might have been but it's not for me. I've told you that there was an occasion when I tried to take myself over, but in the event I died, as all good men should do, in bed. But come back again . . ?' There was a pause before the haughty, arrogant tones switched to the warmth of broad Lancashire ' . . . nay, lass, nay.' And then he was gone. For the last time the director shouted, 'Cut,' and the lights were switched off. Intentionally this time. The temperature in that room had soared to an almost tropical level. I felt like a limp rag. It was a combination of the intense heat and the sheer mental pounding I'd been given by George Orwell. He was, without doubt, one of the most difficult spirits I have ever encountered.

'Come on, John, let's get ourselves a cuppa,' I said. 'I'm jiggered.'

The tv company had thoughtfully provided a room for us for the day and, as I lay on the double bed, I thought back over the day's events.

It struck me that George Orwell was a restless soul in need of prayers and I made a note to include him in mine from now on. And then I thought, maybe when I pass over I'll be able to talk to him face to face. '*Mr* Orwell,' I shall say, 'Don't you dare call me *woman* again. For your information, it's Mrs Stokes. But, just to show there's no hard feelings, you can call me Doris if you like!'

I was still puzzling over who Lucy might be a few days later when I happened to switch on the television. There was a programme about the life of Orwell. It said the scar on his neck was caused by a wound in the Spanish Civil War. The programme also revealed that Orwell and his wife had kept geese. There had been emotional scenes because one of them was due to be slaughtered for Christmas dinner. In the event it had become so much a family pet that its life was spared.

I couldn't contain myself. Almost choking with laughter, I shouted out to John, 'You'll be pleased to know George Orwell isn't completely on his own on the other side.'

'Who's he got with him then?'

'A goose!'

There was a pause, a deep breath, and then John said, 'How do you know?'

' 'Cos they've just explained it on the telly. That Lucy we were looking for in Ipswich was a blinking goose!'

Chapter Eleven

When a journalist asked me what I say to those who suggest I am working with the devil, I told her I tell them, 'I don't know if I am or not, I've never met the devil. Have you?'

Humour is the only way to deal with questions like that. And then I ask them, 'After his crucifixion, did Jesus Christ appear to Mary Magdalene? And didn't he also appear to Doubting Thomas? And didn't Jesus also say, "Everything is possible when done in My Father's name"?'

And when the answer to all these questions is 'Yes, that's true. He did.' I say, 'Well, what's good enough for Jesus Christ is good enough for me!'

I don't get really cross with such people, but I don't really like discussing the subject because I believe religion is something very personal and we all have our own way of finding our way to God. All I know is that I have found it through spiritualism, and I'm pleased I've been able to help a lot of other people along the way. It gives me even more pleasure when I've been able to point out a signpost or two to youngsters just setting out on the road through life.

One of the loveliest letters I received recently came from a young lady, Miss Christina Pentland, who lives in Putney, South London. I'd like to share it with you:

'Dear Doris,
I never believed in anything before I read your

118

books. That was a couple of months ago, just after the twelfth of January when my Nan passed over.

'My Mum's cousin told us about your books, although my Mum has never been a believer in life after death and it seemed to go in one ear and out the other.

'Then her cousin Darren kept on at her and eventually Mum got tickets for one of your sittings. I couldn't go because I'd just come out of hospital after having my tonsils removed and had to stay indoors for two weeks.

'I waited at home, not expecting anything to happen the first time (and neither did Mum) but she came home so excited, telling my Dad and me that Nan had come through.

'Nan had said that I should go to art college, and talked about a coat of my Mum's and so many other things that only our family could have known that it left no room for doubt.

'Blimey, Doris, I've never believed in anything before! I have never even been a great believer in God and I'm still unsure, but now I've read your books I think I'll have a go at the Bible.'

I do love that line, it's given me many a chuckle and a nice warm feeling, but the important thing is that the young lass now believes there may, after all, be some purpose to life. Anyway, the letter ended:

'Well, I just wrote to say thanks, you've helped us a great deal and I just wish I could have some of your specialness.

'Yours admiringly, Christina, aged fifteen years eight months.'

Well, Christina, I don't agree about my being special. As I've said many times, mediums are no different from anyone else. We're all born with the gift, it's just that some of us manage to hang on to it, while others lose it because of pressures from the world. The question I get asked more than any other is, 'how can I become a medium?' There's no easy answer, except to say that if the gift is still with you it can be developed.

I suppose I have been more fortunate than most because my father, Sam Sutton, was a fully-fledged Romany and a natural medium.

If you've read my earlier books you'll know that I was aware of having a gift from a very early age, in fact it's been with me for as long as I can remember and one of my earliest recollections of a glimpse into the spirit world was as a four-year-old when we lived in Grantham.

A neighbour died in a fire and while everybody else stood around in silence as they brought his body out I could see that neighbour as large as life and without a mark on him. He was striding alongside the stretcher which carried his charred remains.

My dad was a genuine Romany and he also had a psychic gift. He was a wise and kindly old soul who knew about my psychic powers too, but poor Mum could never come to terms with it. She used to say that one day I would end up in a mental hospital and she was right. I did later on in life – as a nurse.

Being psychic had enormous advantages. As a child I was never alone. I always had plenty of young friends to play with although looking back I suppose some people must have thought me odd as I was apparently able to amuse myself for hours on end. In fact I was as happy as a sandboy surrounded by playmates that nobody else could see. They were spirit children but to me they were as real as the youngsters I went to school with every day.

I didn't know at that time they were from the spirit world, of course. It was something that at my tender age was beyond my understanding but even so a voice inside me warned that I should be cautious and never mention my friends to anyone else. I somehow realized they might not understand. They would think me 'peculiar' but as far as I was concerned I lived in a lovely world and there was nothing at all strange about it.

In later years when I came to accept that I had this gift I knew that I must develop it but I made quite a few mistakes and took a few wrong turnings up blind alleys before I found myself on the right road.

Looking back now I can say it's a gift which has brought me great personal joy as well as tremendous heartache. It was through my voices, and in particular my late father's, that I learned my beloved husband John had not died when he parachuted into the slaughter of Arnhem during the last war. I knew he was alive and this was despite the fact that the War Office insisted he was dead. They even told me that once the grave numbers were sorted out they would let me know where he was buried. My voices told me otherwise and, as I learned later, John had been wounded and ended up in a Prisoner of War hospital in Holland.

During the dark days of despair as I waited for news of him and before the spirit world brought me that message I grew closer and closer to my five-month-old son, John Michael. I loved him more than I ever thought possible and it was only by having him with me during this time that I retained my sanity.

The news of John's safety was probably the happiest psychic message I've ever received. But imagine my horror when I was then told that my precious baby was to be returned to the spirit world. How could spirits who had been so kind now come with such terrible messages? It was relayed to me by someone who later revealed himself as my spirit guide Ramonov and, five weeks later, just as Ramonov predicted John Michael did pass over. In fact I personally handed him to my father waiting on the other side.

John Michael is now a strapping man in the spirit world but he's still very close to me. The grief of his passing is long since gone although I still miss his physical presence dearly. He does, however, still visit us and he certainly helps keep an eye on our adopted son, Terry.

I often say: 'Please keep an eye on Terry for me, John Michael. You know what he can be like sometimes.' And I know my son hears that message. Only recently I believe he could have intervened to save Terry's life.

Terry's a bus driver and had just finished his shift when the accident happened. He was travelling as a passenger on a bus and was chatting to the conductor. They'd been gossiping for about ten minutes when Terry told him, 'I'm just going to nip upstairs for a smoke.'

It was a split second later, my lad had just turned his head when the bow of a boat – yes, a boat of all things – came tearing through the side of the bus. It caught Terry on the side of the head and his ear was badly gashed. It needed a lot of stitches but as the policemen who investigated the incident later told us it was the nearest anyone is ever likely to come to death without actually passing over.

The boat was being towed by a car which went out of control. Just an eighth of an inch to one side and Terry would have been crushed to death. The fact that he escaped is nothing short of a miracle.

Maybe God had decided that I had lost enough children in my life. Four, including John Michael, have returned to the spirit world and although the agony was hard to bear at the time I gradually came to accept that there is a reason for everything, no matter how cruel it may seem at the time.

To be a good medium you have to understand life and to appreciate life you have to experience suffering. Sometimes it has been hard to reconcile myself to that fact, I'm only human after all, but I can comfort myself with the knowledge that God has given me a gift I must use to help others.

And it's knowing that I can be of help in showing and proving to people there is a life beyond the earth plane, a far better life than we know here and one where all our infirmities and pain disappear, that gives me the strength to continue with my work.

All mediums must find their own way to develop their particular gift and although I was advised the best way for me to do it was by joining a developing circle this just didn't work for me. Developing circles are usually set up by established mediums to help young people with a gift but I developed in my own way. I read every book on spiritualist philosphy I could lay my hands on and eventually I managed to unscramble the voices in my ear. I learned to distinguish between the different ones that came flooding through although it did take a lot of time and patience.

It was all worthwhile in the end though and one of

the proudest moments of my life came at the age of 29 when I received my credentials from the Spiritualist Union. I was a fully fledged medium! Or so I thought at the time. How naive I must have been in those days! Thirty-five years later and I'm still learning.

The best advice I can give to any budding medium just starting out is to remember the three characteristics that you'll always need. They are humility, honesty and humour. The most important part of a medium's training is to learn to put yourself to one side.

You have to ignore your own thoughts and report only what the spirit world is asking you to say. This takes years of practice and there is always the temptation to either put your own interpretation on what comes through or even embellish the messages you receive.

With a medium's honesty I have to say we all make mistakes from time to time – and I'm no exception – but these days I stick strictly to relaying the messages given to me by the voices. With equal honesty I have to confess that my guide Ramonov has told me he won't let me do anything else.

He showed me very early on in my career that I must stick to the rules or else he wouldn't help me. That's why today if I lose a contact while I'm holding a demonstration I'll say 'Let's sing a hymn' or maybe I'll even crack a joke or two until I can establish the link again.

Very occasionally and completely unintentionally I have let my own interpretation come through on a message but you can soon tell because things start to go wrong. Then I'll admit quite openly, 'I've made a right pig's ear of that. Let's clear the vibrations and start again.'

Total honesty and faithful reporting of the messages

is the only way for both your own self respect and for the sake of the people who come to you and one of the nicest compliments ever paid to me by a journalist was the girl from Fleet Street who wrote, 'One of the reasons for Doris's popularity is that she is never afraid to admit when she's made a mistake.'

I don't know about the reason for popularity but yes, I'll own up to my mistakes because I know I'll get in an awful mess if I don't but sometimes of course it's not my fault. Even the spirit world can get things wrong or muddled up. They may not be human any more but just because a spirit is now on the other side there is no reason for them to change. We don't suddenly become super intelligent.

Whenever I hold a seminar for potential mediums I tell them they must learn to trust their guide and not question them too much. And also whenever you have a quiet moment or last thing at night sit down and offer yourself in service to God. That's most important because that's what it is all about. All the answers you need to know will come in time. It took ten years before my guide told me anything about himself. I wasn't too bothered. It was sufficient for me to know that he was with me and helping me.

We've all got a guide, of course. They are souls who elect to come back to earth to help guide us through our earthly cycle and when we pass over they come with us. Sometimes you'll hear someone say they now have the guide of some famous medium who's passed on but I don't believe this can be so. When you pass over your guide continues on his or her own progression. They certainly don't come back for a second stint.

I was actually watching television when I learnt more about my guide. There was a trailer for a programme called, *Tibet, the Roof of the World* when a voice said to me, 'That's where I came from. That's where I lived on the earth plane.' It turned out that Ramonov had been a priest and a very wise one at that. I once asked him while doing my meditation, 'I'm getting on a bit now you know. Do you think you could give me any idea when I'll be coming over?'

He replied: 'You'll have enough time to do the work God has chosen you to do.'

And it was the right answer, I thought to myself. If I knew when my time was up I'd probably not bother chasing round the country trying to help other people.

I might just say to myself, 'Well, I'm about to die so I better lay myself up somewhere and take it easy.' So I live every day as it comes and try to cram as much into it as possible.

I also believe in giving the youngsters a chance in mediumship although they should forget any nonsense about glamour or mystery. It's sheer hard work and many times I warn them they'll be up against prejudice, abuse and the accusations of being a fake. It's not an easy life, it requires dedication, and I remember one night asking Ramonov despairingly, 'D'you think I'll ever be any good at this?'

His reply is something I repeat to all budding mediums and it's sound advice to all of us, whether or not we have a psychic gift.

Ramonov told me, 'Picture to yourself a mountain and upon the top of this mountain there stands a shrine. Now I tell you, my children, every one of us has come this way before you. None of us can say we'll ever reach the shrine on the earth plane but as long as you keep aiming for it, that is all that matters.

'You will set off up the pathway and it will all seem easy and you'll think what's all the fuss about? I can do it. Then you will come to a place which will be filled with many people of many colours and many creeds, and you will stop and you will ask, "what are they doing here?" You will be told that this is the half-way house. Nobody will blame you if you decide to stay there but by the same token your development will also stay there.

'Now the second half of the climb, for every step you take you will fall back. You will fall and bruise your knees but I say again every one of us has trodden the same pathway before you. We cannot promise you roses all the way. We cannot even promise to remove the stones from the pathway.

'What I can promise is that I will always be there to take your hand when you have to climb a stone, and always say to yourself "One day I will reach the shrine." '

It was a beautiful story and it has spurred me on to aim for the top, no matter how discouraging things may be at times. We might not all make it but we'll never know until we try and from what Ramonov has told me I think it's worth having a go!

Another piece of advice I offer to young mediums and anyone else interested in spiritualism is to forget the ouija board. It will only attract mishievous or earthbound spirits. They're the sort who refuse to accept they have passed on. You know the type. They say, 'If I can't take it with me then I'm not going.' They hate to let go of worldly possessions and it's these poor souls we need to pray for to help them over properly.

Quite often they are the people who are insistent that there is no life after death so when it happens they won't accept it even then. They won't even listen to their guide. They tell themselves, 'Look, I've got a body. There's nothing wrong with me.' So they stay earthbound until they are helped by prayer or until someone they love also passes over and tells them, 'Look, luv, accept you've passed over. There's something better ahead so just move on!'

The other world in fact is only the blink of an eye away and if you have the gift of mediumship all you have to do is open your heart, send out love and this will act as a chain which will link you with those in the world beyond. Don't be scared. The spirit world is full of people like you and me. It's full of our relatives and friends who have passed on. They don't change so if you weren't frightened of them on earth there's certainly no need to be frightened of them on the other side.

Too often people like to wrap it up in all sorts of mumbo jumbo but contact with the other side comes through harmony and love combined with the humility which every medium must learn. Once you have that you can tune in but if you can do that you've also got to accept the responsibility that goes with it. But forget the mumbo jumbo. I hear people talk about chakras. They tell me it's some point of the body which can tune into the other side. I don't know if I've got one or not. I certainly don't know where it is. All I do know is that at the end of a sitting my solar plexus aches and I'm exhausted. If I don't feel like that then I don't think I've worked hard enough. But I know of one medium who flew out to Switzerland to give a very wealthy businessman a 'consultation'. That's what the posh mediums call their sittings. He'd been flown out at the businessman's expense and was chauffer-driven from the airport to a very swish house up in the mountains.

The medium also reckoned himself to be a bit of a healer too. After the 'consultation' he told the businessman he had a torn chakra but never mind, the medium had at great personal mental effort managed

128

to insert some stitches in it. He would of course have to be flown back to Switzerland again in six weeks time so that he could take them out! And what's more the businessman believed him!

Maybe there *is* something in this chakra business but I've never needed one myself as far as I know. I've got a humble soul for a spirit guide and a simple philosophy on how to chat with the other side. And it works. I should say though that once you do manage to tune in you have to make sure the spirit world doesn't rule you. Believe me, if you let them, they'd take over night and day and use you twenty-four hours at a time. I can't really blame them for trying. After all there are so many spirits who want to get in touch with their loved ones here to reassure them that everything's all right and that there is something to look forward to when they pass over.

But a medium must learn to say, 'No, not just now, luv. I'm tired and I've finished for the day. Come back tomorrow.' There has to be a point when you close down the lines of communication for the night – or you could end up with a cerebral haemorrhage and that would result in a permanent disconnection!

Chapter Twelve

The mist had lifted earlier in the day from Southampton Water and throughout the afternoon the city had been basking in the warm, early spring sunshine. There was also a spring in the walk of the shoppers and a sense of expectancy in the air. Winter was over and all round nature was waking up again.

There was also a feeling of anticipation at the home of Denise Johnson, some five miles from the city centre. Her husband Derek is a salesman who's done quite well for himself. A new car and a smart new detached house in what estate agents call a 'highly desirable area'.

They are a very happily married couple who enjoy life to the full in almost every respect. Just one tragedy twelve years ago has marred an otherwise idyllic partnership. And it was something that Derek has refused to talk about ever since.

Denise, as much in love with her husband as the day they married fourteen years ago, found this heartbreaking. She didn't let her feeling show, however, but decided their marriage was more important than Derek's attitude to one incident however important it might be to herself. Over the years, Denise had managed to hide her own feelings behind a mask of cheerful efficiency. She had done it so well that none of their neighbours ever guessed at the underlying torment she felt. If Derek knew, he didn't show it. His attitude had remained consistent over the years: it was something he had completely blotted out of his mind.

In every other respect, as Denise never ceased telling everybody, Derek was a model husband and a doting father to their two young children.

All this I knew nothing about when I visited Southampton where *An Evening With Doris Stokes* had been arranged at the Civic Centre.

I've promised Denise that I won't use her real name, but everything I'm going to tell you has been faithfully recorded. Indeed, much of the information was volunteered by Denise when she contacted me following that evening in the Civic Centre.

It began when Denise spotted an advertisement for the demonstration in the local evening paper. She mentioned it casually to her husband, who scoffed and said, 'I've got better things to do with my time than to go and listen to that lot.'

He knew why Denise had mentioned it but he had long since buried all thoughts of the tragedy deep in the recesses of his mind. Or so he thought. His unusually abrupt and mocking attitude towards his wife showed that it was far from forgotten. Like so many other people, he was afraid to inquire about the spirit world.

For once, however, Denise was determined to stand her ground. She said, 'It may be a waste of time for you but I'm going.'

Derek didn't reply. Nor did he offer to drive his wife into town to buy her ticket.

It didn't deter Denise. Nor did his sullen silence on that sunny afternoon shortly before the demonstration. Never having been to anything like this before, she wasn't quite sure what to wear. Twice she changed her outfit before she was satisfied with the result. Then, turning to her husband, she said, 'Would you mind taking me into town?'

Derek replied, 'I'll drop you off, but you can find your own way home.'

It was completely out of character for the warm and loving family man, but Denise recognized it as his last desperate attempt to stop her from going.

'All right, darling, I'll find my own way home. And now, please, would you mind running me into town.'

As Denise said later, 'To say that the atmosphere was cold in the car would be putting if mildly. I could almost see the icicles forming.'

Derek spoke only once during the journey, just as his wife was getting out of the car. It was in a mocking tone. 'Enjoy yourself with the ghosts.'

Denise had said nothing in reply, but headed towards the theatre balcony. Vaguely, she was hoping for proof of something or other. But if anyone had stopped her she wouldn't have known what to tell them. Nor would she have been able to give any logical explanation as to why she was risking an almighty row with her husband. That was something she had taken great pains to avoid for years.

Backstage at about the same time I was nervously preparing myself for the demonstration. The previous twenty-four hours had been fairly eventful. In the morning, before leaving for Southampton, John and I were having breakfast when we heard a thud on the landing outside our flat. We dashed out to find one of the residents in our block lying dead on the floor.

After the ambulance had taken his body away, I happened to remark to a neighbour, 'What a wonderful way to go.'

She looked shocked and said, 'What a terrible thing to say!'

I replied gently: 'No, it isn't. We shouldn't be feeling

sorry for him. He's passed over with no trouble at all.' What everyone saw lying out there was just an old, discarded overcoat. His spirit has gone on to better things.

'There's no need to feel sorry, on his behalf. It's his wife we should care about now, she needs the help and comfort. Her husband is free from all the aches and pains of this world.'

I can understand people's fear of death, but as I've said on many occasions: You can't die for the life of you! The spirit is immortal and life beyond this world a far better experience. Perhaps, if I related what had happened on that balcony at home, it might help others in the audience who have this fear of death.

I tune in before every demonstration, but until I'm actually out on stage I never know what I'm going to say or what is going to happen. Talking about the death at our block of flats would be a good way to start the evening until the messages began coming through.

So as soon as I walked on the stage, I explained what had happened on the balcony and how spiritualism taught me never to fear the afterlife. Then I remembered a message that came to me as John and I were travelling down to Southampton.

I had glanced out of the car window as our driver was overtaking another vehicle. The letters on the numberplate spelled out FRY and a man's voice in my head said, 'It's Wayne Fry. My wife met you four years ago. Her name's Vivienne. Give her my love.'

I looked around the audience. I could see no blue light, but nevertheless I mentioned what the voice had told me. A young man jumped up from a seat near the centre aisle and said, 'Vivienne's my sister, Doris!'

'Did Wayne own a restaurant?' I asked.

'Yes!'

133

'Well, we've got the right one. Just tell Vivienne he sends her his love.' And then, without thinking, I added, 'They weren't married long were they?'

The young man replied, 'No, they weren't. Only fourteen months.'

The contact was there but Vivienne wasn't and suddenly Wayne moved aside to allow a flood of spirit messages to come through. The first was from a young girl, Rachel Kelly, who told me her name and address and then promptly started to sing 'Happy Birthday'. I explained what I had heard and then I saw the light hovering over a couple on the other side of the auditorium. The man stood up and said, 'That's our daughter, Doris. It was her birthday yesterday.'

'Give Michael my love,' said Rachel.

'That's her brother,' exclaimed Mrs Kelly.

'Tell Mummy I didn't suffer. I was killed you know, Doris.' Rachel was excited now that she'd got through to her parents. She went on, 'They managed to reach me but I'd already gone. I could see them standing by my body but I wasn't there. It's hard to explain.'

But Mr and Mrs Kelly didn't need any explanation. The accuracy of the message from little Rachel was enough to prove their daughter was now well again and living happily in the spirit world.

By now there were a dozen blue lights over the auditorium and messages were coming thick and fast. It wasn't until almost the end of the evening that I saw a strong and steady blue light up on the balcony, and a boy's voice said, 'My name's Simon and I want to be up there.'

I pointed to the blur of a face over which the clear light hovered:

134

'Have you got a Simon in the spirit world?'

'Yes.'

Still I couldn't see the face, and the voice was unsteady.

I said, 'Well, luv, can you come down here? You're too far away up there. I don't think it's fair when your loved ones have taken the trouble to come through. I like to be close so they can be near you too.'

And that's how, a minute or so later, I came face to face for the first time with Denise Johnson. I could see immediately that she had just gone through a severe emotional shock. I asked, 'Do you want to compose yourself for a little while, darling?'

She looked bewildered and just stared without replying. I said as gently as I could, 'Don't get yourself upset, pet. It's only Doris.'

Denise gulped and managed to stammer: 'I, I'm all right.'

The voice in my ear was insistent that I give her the message. He was a child and he was excited. I said, 'It's only a very young voice and he's saying to me. "I'm Simon and I want to be up on the balcony." He knew you were there.' Momentarily I felt a pain which made me gasp. I said, "Darling, I can't get my breath." That's what happened, isn't it?'

There was a flood of tears as Denise sobbed, 'Yes. He was a blue baby, only twelve hours old.'

Simon said, 'Tell her not to cry, Doris. It's my Mum. Tell her I'm growing up now. I'm getting to be a big boy.'

I relayed the message and then asked Simon, 'Is Mummy alone?'

He replied: 'No, I've got a sister, and then there's Billie.'

'Who's Billie?' I asked Denise.

135

'That's what they call my eldest son,' said Denise. Her voice was clearer now. There were no tears, but now more a sort of wonderment.

Simon laughed and said, 'She never thought I'd come through to her. Just mention fishing and say Dekka. That'll cheer her up.'

I said: 'He's talking about fishing. And who's Dekka?'

Denise looked as if someone had just put two thousand volts through her. Her hair almost stood on end. Then she gasped, 'That's my husband's nickname. And he's keen on fishing.'

I could hear Simon chuckle in my ear as he said gently, 'Tell her not to cry for me again, Doris. I'm all right.'

But Simon could see that from his mother's face. The sparkling eyes and the beaming smile from ear to ear told its own story.

As a parting message, Simon said, 'Let her know, Doris, that I could tell she couldn't make up her mind what to wear. She changed her outfit before coming out you know.'

When I relayed this to Denise, she simply squealed with joy. Later, when she had recovered from the shock, she explained to a journalist what had led her to Southampton Civic Centre that evening:

'It was twelve years ago when we lost Simon and he was only twelve hours old. It was traumatic, having gone through a full pregnancy only to have a life ended so quickly and cruelly.

'It hurt me deeply, but it hurt my husband even more than he realized. He went to the funeral and then brooded for weeks. After that he refused to acknowledge his son had ever existed. The subject was banned.

'At first I used to try and make him talk about it.

I felt that we both needed to, it would have been therapeutic, but Derek just wouldn't listen.

'Whenever I tried to mention Simon's name he'd either fly into a rage, clam up completely or just storm out of the house. Eventually I gave up trying to talk to him about it.

'We've now got two other children and as the years have passed even I was beginning to wonder if Simon had ever existed. Had he been a figment of my own imagination?

'It was frightening. Derek had tried to brainwash us both into believing it was a tragedy that never happened. But deep down, of course, I knew this was nonsense. I have felt Simon's presence, I don't know how, but I've felt he's been around. And yet I've never known what to do about it. This helplessness almost drove me to despair at times.

'I'd heard of Doris, but never read any of her books and only had a vague idea of what spiritualism was all about. When I went into that hall I'd no real idea what I was looking for. Certainly it wasn't a message from my son. I was just hoping there might be some sort of proof that there is a meaning to life.

'When Simon came through I have to admit I was completely floored. It was the most incredible experience of my life. Even now, days later, I tremble when I think about it. The accuracy of the messages left me in no doubt as to their authenticity. The things he said were known to nobody else in that hall. I didn't know anybody else at all there. I was entirely alone.

'On the way home afterwards I wondered how I was going to break what had happened to Derek. I decided to say nothing at all. I had visions of him rushing me off to the nearest hospital and insisting on my head being examined.

'But when I got home I just burst into tears. Somehow, I found the strength to tell him, "I know you're not going to believe this, but you're jolly well going to sit down and hear me out whether you like it or not. And I don't give a damn if you think I'm crazy."

'His reaction wasn't at all what I'd expected. He just sat listening, dumbfounded. Then we sat up half the night trying to puzzle it all out.

'I know even then my husband wasn't fully convinced. He rang up a close relative and asked if we could come over and talk. Our relative then disclosed that she was a spiritualist, but because of her job she'd never told anybody. She said she believed every word I had said. And every message from Doris.

'This just floored Derek. I know now, for a fact, he's been out and bought Doris's books and he's secretly reading them. I haven't mentioned Simon again, but I have a feeling it won't be long before Derek does.

'There'll be no question of us discussing him at any length or on many occasions. But as long as Derek acknowledges he has a son who is now in the spirit world, I'll be happy. And I know Simon will be too.

'It will happen. I can tell. There's a different atmosphere in the house – and that atmosphere isn't just because Simon's around watching over us.'

Chapter Thirteen

I've appeared in so many radio and television studios round the country in the past twelve months that I think I'll soon be due for my union card. I'm not often paid, but when I am the fee goes straight to the Save the Children Fund.

One of the inverviews I remember best was with Ed Doolan. He's a bright and chirpy Australian, who's got his own show with BBC WM, a radio station in Birmingham, but we first met when Ed was working for a rival radio station.

It was obvious when they ushered me into the studio on that first occasion that Ed had never met a medium before. He's a very professional journalist and, like a lot of Australians, Ed doesn't stand any nonsense. But I could see straight away that he felt uneasy with me.

The producer sat me down opposite Ed and adjusted the microphone. The poor lad looked distinctly uncomfortable and, as he admitted to me later, at that time he'd never heard of me or read my books.

The programme was going out live and I heard the producer say, 'Thirty seconds to go.' I glanced across at Ed again. He obviously wasn't very happy, so I said, 'You're concerned, luv, aren't you?'

Ed nodded in agreement, adding, 'Well, yes, I mean you're talking to people on the other side and I've got people on the other side.'

'There's no need to worry,' I replied. 'Your Dad's here with us as well. His name's Ed too and he's very proud of you.'

Ed nearly fell off his chair with shock! But, true professional that he is, he managed to control himself beautifully. We went on air a few seconds later without a hitch and the programme was a huge success.

Since that first interview we've become friends and I was again a guest on Ed's programme on this recent tour. He acted as chairman at the first of the demonstrations I held at the Odeon in Birmingham. He recounted our first meeting and almost had me blushing when he told the audience, 'It was one of the most moving and exciting moments of my life.'

You don't expect compliments like that from handsome young men when you get to my age!

As we went on stage there was a demonstration of a different kind going on outside the theatre, but Ed handled it beautifully. As everybody came into the Odeon, a pamphlet was thrust into their unwilling hands. Ed held his up high and said, 'I've got a leaflet here, have you?'

There was a rousing cry of 'Yes!'

He replied, 'Mine says "What is going on in here is in direct disobedience to God." If I'd known that you would all have been charged more!' As I've said before, it's silly to take such demonstrations against spiritualism seriously.

The only time I'm ever hurt is when people say I'm a fake. No matter how hard I prove otherwise, there are always people around who just will not accept that I'm honestly trying my best. And that really does upset me. Mind you, the first time I heard the accusation my reaction was pretty drastic.

The number has no significance, but it was thirteen years after I had received my credentials from the Spiritualists' Union. And they had been thirteen years in which I had been happily engrossed in my work as a medium. I was then 42 years old and I overheard the remark as I was leaving a spiritualist meeting in London. A woman said, 'Isn't she good!'

Her companion replied, 'Oh, she's not genuine. She must have looked up names in the telephone book or something. She's much too good to be genuine.'

I was mortified. I could hardly believe my ears and I was so upset it didn't occur to me to reply. I just rushed past them, my eyes blinded by tears, wanting to get away from the place as quickly as possible. How could anybody say such a thing? And how many other people were saying it out of earshot?

At that time John was working as a porter at the Royal Albert Hospital. I raced down the street, frantically looking for the nearest telephone box. If that's what people thought of me, I knew exactly what I was going to do. I telephoned the hospital and asked to speak to the Matron.

'Are there any vacancies?' I said.

It was a mental hospital and in a mental hospital there are always vacancies, so I was taken on straight away. And that was how, at the age of 46, four years later, I became a fully-fledged State Enrolled Nurse. If it hadn't been for a subsequent violent attack by a patient, which left me without a thyroid gland, and an increasing number of other health problems, who knows, maybe I would have stayed there until I was due for retirement. But somehow I doubt it. I don't think Ramonov would have allowed it. He would have had me back in harness again, doing the work I was doing that evening in Birmingham. And the work I know I was born to do.

On this current tour I visited Birmingham four times, and on the first occasion, like the others, the seats were sold out at least a week in advance. I looked out at a sea of more than 2,000 friendly faces and thought to myself, 'What does it matter what some people say? Don't let it get you down.' But deep down inside it still hurts.

As we settled down for the first demonstration, I asked, as usual, why people had come to see me. A fair number had read my previous books and this had made them want to see me in person. Very flattering, of course, but then came other reasons: curiosity, interest, hope. And it is this last reason that sums up a lot of what I do. I do my utmost to bring hope to people, by proving there is something worthwhile at the end of it all.

Certainly I knew during the question and answer session I brought hope to one young woman. She was auburn-haired and wore a worried look on her pale face. It seemed to me she had been crying a lot.

The spirit world told me her name was Noreen Maitland and that she had lost both her parents within the past three years.

'My Mum was ever so religious but Dad wasn't, Doris,' she said. 'Mum went to church every week and prayed a lot. Dad did neither but he was good to his family. He really was a wonderful man.'

'Well, what's the problem, luv?'

She was about to break into tears. 'People tell me they won't be in the same place together, and yet I know Dad loved her so much,' she sobbed.

'Rubbish!' I shouted, so loudly into the microphone that I almost deafened myself. But people who say that sort of thing do make me mad.

'It sounds to me as if your Dad was a very good man indeed. You don't have to be on your knees praying all day to prove you're good. And you don't have to do it in church. God is everywhere.'

Suddenly I saw the outline of a man sitting in front of a black and white board. And a voice whispered in my ear. I said, 'Does your Dad play chess or draughts, luv?'

Noreen's face lit up and she beamed. 'He loved playing draughts, Doris. He played with us almost every night.'

I replied, 'Well he's still at it, luv, and he's just said to me, "Doris, if this is Hell, I'll have a double dose of it!"'

The next questioner was a girl no more than 23 years old. Dark black hair and again her face was etched with lines of grief. There were two babies with her, a boy and girl, each about two years old. But although everybody in the Odeon could see the young woman, I realized the babies were spirits. In fact, I knew instantly they were twins who had twice tried to make contact earlier in the demonstration with someone in the audience. I didn't need telling who this sad young woman was, but I said nothing until she asked me quietly, 'Doris, why are babies taken away from us?' She was their mother.

Why are babies taken away from us, especially at birth – as I knew was the case with this young girl – is a question I've been asked many times and one which I too have asked a hundred times over having been through it all myself.

I gave her my answer and told her that one day she would be reunited with those babies so painfully wrenched from her, while her spirit children listened intently. I'm sure I could see them nodding in agreement, although I know that even two-year-old spirit children aren't that wise!

Then the little boy whispered to me: 'Tell Mummy

143

we love her, Doris, and now we've got names. I'm Simon and my sister's called Laurie.'

I asked the young woman: 'Did you name your children, luv?'

'No, Doris, they were stillborn.'

'A boy and a girl?'

'Yes,' she said in surprise.

'Well, let me tell you, they're not dead. They're here with me now and they want you to know they've been given the names Simon and Laurie.'

Then I asked, 'Have you got any more children, my luv?'

'No,' The answer was emphatic.

'Well, you're expecting one then, aren't you?'

There was a puzzled look on her face. Then she laughed and said, 'Not as far as I know, Doris, but thanks anyway and you really have cheered me up. I always thought I could feel the presence of the twins. Other people said it was my imagination but now I know it isn't.'

And with that she went back to her seat in the audience.

It was five months later when I received the following letter. It was written on bright blue paper with a drawing of Snoopy the dog dancing for joy in the bottom left-hand corner – and no wonder!

Highgate
Birmingham
9 March 1984

Dear Doris,

I hope you are keeping well, and your husband too. May God bless you both.

I came to see you in Birmingham last October.

144

I was the one who asked the question about stillborn children.

At the beginning of the show you said there were twins in spirit and later you said they belonged to me.

You also told me there was another one on the way and I said I didn't think so.

Well, Doris, I can confirm that I am now five months pregnant and I'm looking forward to seeing my baby so much. I want everybody to know this so we can shout out that mediumship is not a lot of old rubbish!

I'd also like you to know that I'm now attending a spiritualist church and I enjoy it very much.

All my love,
Janette Watkins.

Something else rather wonderful happened in Birmingham, this time on Ed Doolin's BBC phone-in.

At that time the Independent Broadcasting Authority had decided there were to be no live demonstrations by mediums on either radio or television – one wonderful recording I did for Granada Television is still waiting to be shown – but Independent radio and television's loss was the BBC's gain, and they were only too happy to invite me on air.

The calls on Ed's show came thick and fast and, although it's extremely difficult to hold a proper sitting when you can't see the person you're talking to, we managed to raise quite a few contacts.

But there was one voice in my head that just wouldn't go away. The message was rather vague but it was so insistent I felt that I had to give it out. If it was picked up, all well and good. If not, then at least I had done my best.

I had no surname but the message came from someone called Rose in the spirit world, the mother of a girl called Maureen.

The only other clue I could offer on air was that Maureen was the mother of twins and her husband's name was John. Rose didn't give me any more information but just said, 'Doris, you've got to tell her to get herself to a healer. It's very urgent.'

Rose's voice sounded so agitated I simply repeated the message as it came to me, interrupting someone else who had just phoned in to ask me a question. To that listener I now apologize, but I think she'll forgive me – especially when I tell her about the letter I received four months later.

Bacons End
Birmingham
3 March

Dear Doris Stokes,

I feel I must write to you to tell you something that I feel will be of interest because it concerns you.

During one of your broadcasts you said you had an urgent message to convey to someone who might be listening in. The message was from a lady in spirit named Rose who was the mother of Maureen. You advised Maureen to seek the help of a spiritual healer urgently because she was very ill, and from other information you gave I have no doubt as to Maureen's identity. I am a spiritual healer and have been for fourteen years. By a strange coincidence Maureen's sister-in-law was coming to me for healing and during the week of your broadcast she asked me if I would see Maureen.

146

She did not think I would be able to give much help because Maureen had only been given six months to live by the doctors at the hospital. She was suffering from cancer.

To cut a long story short, Maureen has been completely cured, much to the amazement of the doctors. It proves yet again that our spirit friends help us in times of need and will go to great lengths to get the message across to us.

God bless you,
Yours very sincerely
Betty Thompson.

God bless you too, Betty, for restoring Maureen to full health once again! But let Betty herself tell you how this miracle came about.

'Maureen's sister just happened to mention to me that she was very ill. Maureen herself didn't believe in spiritualism or healing.

'Her sister, who was obviously very worried, asked me, "Do you think, Betty, if I could persuade her to come along, you could take her on as a patient?"

'I replied: "Of course I will, I'm prepared to help anyone I can."

'I thought no more of it, but a week later, much to my surprise, in walked Maureen. It became evident very quickly that she had a malignant cancer, but within a month she had responded wonderfully to treatment. The growth disappeared.

'Like many other people Maureen was highly sceptical at first, but she was so desperate she was prepared to try anything – at least that's what I thought.

'It was only after we had become friends she admitted that she heard Doris's message on the radio and knew instantly it was meant for her. Even so, Maureen had no intention of revealing this until she had convinced herself about the truth of it all. And there's no doubt about it, as Maureen herself says, she's been given the best possible evidence in the saving of her own life.'

Chapter Fourteen

Smoke brought tears to my eyes and caught in the back of my throat. The crackling of burning timber turned into a roar as the fire took hold and turned the staircase into a raging torrent of flames. But strangely I felt no pain as I slipped into unconsciousness. The scene was so vivid the taste and smell almost engulfed me. In fact I found myself glancing round just to make sure everything was all right.

It was, of course. I was sitting in our flat in Fulham, telephone in hand, and talking to a lovely Geordie called Sam Hayden, who was nearly 300 miles away up in Newcastle. We were holding a sitting following something that Sam says has changed his whole life.

The story began a week earlier when I was in Newcastle giving a demonstration at the City Hall.

It was a chilly and windy April evening but there really is nothing to beat spiritual central heating! And there was plenty of it that night in Newcastle. The warmth coming from that hall was marvellous!

As I arrived, unknown to me Sam Hayden and his brother Raymond were taking their seats in the gallery.

They had desperately wanted to come along and had only got tickets at the last minute from a friend. I wasn't the only medium the Haydens were interested in talking to. They had travelled the length and breadth of the country over the past seven years searching for someone who could help. So far it had been fruitless, and the years of grieving were now threatening to overwhelm the family, especially Sam.

But it was, on the whole, a light-hearted evening for everyone, except the Haydens. They watched and listened glumly as the messages came through thick and fast. They saw the looks of joy on the faces of people sitting round them and heard the laughter as men, women and children who had passed over shared jokes with their loved ones here on the earth plane. There was plenty of love and humour but it wasn't enough to lift the burden of despair from the shoulders of Raymond and Sam.

Then, twenty minutes from the end of the demonstration, I heard a voice saying, 'Give our love to Carl, Doris.' The message was faint and then I heard another name – Janet.

I said, 'It's a bit faint but has anybody got a Carl and a Janet? They're not spirit side.'

From the balcony there was a strangled shout of, 'Here, Doris! Here!'

I couldn't see anything from such a distance, so I asked whoever it was that thought Janet and Carl belonged to them to come down in front of the stage.

A few minutes later there was a middle-aged gentleman standing in front of me, tears of joy streaming down his face. He was so emotional he found it hard to talk, let alone hold the microphone. It was Raymond Hayden. But Raymond had at least done better than Sam. Poor Sam was so shocked his legs turned to jelly and he couldn't get out of his seat! He was still sitting on the balcony, and that's where he stayed until the end of the demonstration!

Raymond managed to blurt out, 'I've got a Janet living. My wife and daughter are both called that, and Carl's my nephew.'

I looked at Raymond and immediately I was sharing the despair they had felt until this very minute.

I said: 'Oh, dear God, there's a great deal of tragedy. I can feel it.'

And there had been. Almost eight years ago, fifteen-year-old John Hayden and his brother Alan, who was a year younger, had died together. At this stage I got nothing more through about the circumstances of their death, but both lads were now trying to talk together. One voice said: 'Carl's our brother, Doris!'

The second chimed in, 'That's our Uncle Ray.' The first interrupted to say, 'Shut up, Alan, I'll do the talking!'

That last remark rang so true to Uncle Raymond that he couldn't contain himself. He was shuddering, and his voice was breaking with emotion as he asked, 'Are they all right, Doris?'

It was John who answered. 'Tell them we're all right now, Doris, but let's talk later. The whole family have spent years trying to get through to us, please let's talk later.'

It was one of the most highly emotional contacts I'd had on this tour, and it was obvious that Alan and John wanted to speak to their father, Sam Hayden, personally.

I told Raymond, 'Look, luv, leave your telephone number and I promise I'll ring you when I get back to London. I'll also ring Alan and John's Dad and we'll have a good old natter. But the boys would rather we do it in private.

'I know there's been seven years of heartache, Raymond, but please believe this, the sun does shine again. I know because I've lost four children. I know that you think happiness is something you or your brother will never experience again, but it isn't true. I'll prove it. I'll ring you next Saturday afternoon from my home.'

From up in the balcony, Sam Hayden had at last found his voice. He shouted down, 'Please do, Doris, please do!'

Raymond turned away from the stage, and in his broad Tyneside accent said, 'If she says she'll phoon, there's noo doot aboot it, she will!' And I did, naturally, but before I made that call I got another lovely surprise.

The following morning I had been invited to sign copies of my earlier books at a shop in Newcastle.

A bubbly woman, with a sparkle in her eyes and a grin that went from ear to ear, placed a beautiful bunch of carnations on the table in front of me and said, 'Doris, I just want to say thanks. I'm Sam Hayden's second wife and I want you to know that he's changed overnight. He's started to live again.'

The following Saturday I made that phone call from Fulham and the full story emerged. The smoke and the flames that I could smell and hear had claimed the lives of the brothers.

The whole tragedy unfolded before me as I listened to Alan and John and relayed the messages Sam had waited so long to hear. John said: 'Please tell Dad that everything is all right now and he mustn't blame himself. There was nothing anyone could do. Uncle Ray's also got to stop torturing himself. We're fine now and we didn't feel a thing. The smoke got to us long before the fire. There's no way anyone could have saved us.'

Alan and John had been sleeping upstairs in the large old house while Sam and his wife, along with brother Carl, the inital contact, were in bed downstairs. The boys had come home about 9.30 pm after spending the day at some stables owned by their Uncle Ray.

He explained: 'I idolized those lads as if they were my own two. I was the last one to see them alive and, ever since, their faces have haunted me. They were my pride and joy.

'Nobody knows how the fire started, but knowing wouldn't have helped anyway. We would like everyone to know how Doris has helped us though. It might only make a page in the book, while Sam has lost a whole chapter of his life, but that's all behind us now. There's a new beginning for all of us.'

And after our little chat on the phone Sam told a journalist:

'The evening that changed our lives began as a surprise. We'd given up hope getting tickets for Doris's demonstration when a friend rang out of the blue to offer us his.

'The initial contact was enough to convince me that Alan and John had come through, but in our telephone conversation Doris said things that nobody outside the family could possibly have known about.

'As a result of what has happened I'm a changed man. In the past I've kept this tragedy bottled up inside me but now I don't mind talking about it. The uplift I feel is tremendous, quite simply I can face life again.

'Ever since the funeral, my sons have had the nicest graves in the cemetery. I had flowers brought in specially from Holland once a fortnight to put on those graves but now I realize the boys aren't resting six feet underground. They're not in the cemetery, they're here with us.

'We've got two photographs of the boys in the living room and I put the flowers there now. Every day I smile at those photographs and say "Good morning." And every evening before I go to bed I make sure I say "goodnight."

'They were more than my lads. They were my pals, and my world just ended after that fire. But I realize now they're not dead and gone. Their spirits are with us all the time, living and loving alongside us. Now that I have seen this my own life has begun again.'

Chapter Fifteen

They'd never seen a performance like it in the Philharmonic Hall in Liverpool. And neither had I. It was another happy evening on tour and tonight the spirit world had come up with a new line in providing evidence.

I had just contacted a young woman's grandmother when the number 'eleven' came through loud and clear. I asked, 'Does that mean anything to you, luv?'

She paused a second or two and then laughed. 'It's the number of my seat, Doris.' A few minutes later I was contacting somebody else's brother-in-law when a voice in my ear gave the number 'sixteen'.

'What does that mean?' I asked. 'That's *my* seat number, Doris!' There was a gust of laughter right round the hall. At least it shows the spirit world also has a sense of humour.

While this was happening I was conscious of someone watching me from the side of the stage. John always sits there through every demonstration, but I could sense there was somebody standing behind him. I glanced over and saw a young policeman, complete with helmet. A few minutes later I glanced over again. And now I could see two of them.

Earlier in the evening there had been a demonstration outside the theatre by a handful of people who objected to my visit. I thought to myself, 'Well I know some people don't quite know what to make of me, but there was no need to call in the law!'

Then there was a crackled message on one policeman's walkie-talkie radio and both vanished. Fortunately, I didn't see what happened next or I should have been in a right old panic, but apparently they returned about five minutes later.

And this time they'd brought eight of their pals with them! John said it looked really comical seeing ten policemen in a row all straining their ears to catch every word. One of them said, 'I told you she was good, didn't I!' Then there was another message on a walkie-talkie and they all trooped out again. We later discovered that the hall was opposite one of the main police stations in Liverpool and, obviously, a few minutes of *An Evening With Doris Stokes* was better than sitting in the police canteen.

We had a marvellous reception and everyone we met in Liverpool was lovely and did everything possible to make us feel at home. And there's another reason why I've got a soft spot for Merseyside: a gurgling little bundle of fun called Daniel and a story that goes back to when I first visited the city twelve months previously.

It was at a book signing in a city centre shop on a summer's day so hot that it was almost drying the ink in my pen. I looked up from the desk at which I was sitting and along a queue which, by now, stretched out of the front door of the shop and down the street. Half way along the queue stood a young woman, obviously heavily pregnant. She wasn't complaining, but I could see she was distressed by the heat. I said, 'Come on forward, my luv, let's not keep you waiting.' Everyone else in the queue was quite happy to let her through and she put a book in front of me, saying, 'Thank you, Doris, I don't think I could have stood it much longer.'

Almost without realizing what I was saying, I blurted out, 'How does the name Daniel sound?'

She looked startled for a second and then said, 'Why that's a lovely name, Doris! If it's a boy that's what we'll call him.'

Again without thinking, I replied, 'Daniel he will be.' A few months later I received a letter from that young lady. Her name is Lynda Matthews from Seaforth, just outside Liverpool. The letter read:

> 'Dear Doris,
>   I hope you still remember me. We met in a shop last year and now I've got Daniel with me!'

And that was why, a few hours before I went on stage at the Philharmonic Hall that day, twenty-five of us were gathered in an hotel suite in Liverpool for Daniel's naming ceremony – the nearest thing in the Spiritualist Church to a christening. The main difference is that we don't believe a baby is born with any sin, so there's no water needed to wash it away. Instead, we have pure white flowers to symbolise the little mite's purity and innocence.

A journalist from the Liverpool evening paper had heard about the ceremony and asked if she could come along too. Why not? It's a lovely service and we'd like more people to know about spiritualism. But it all came as a bit of a surprise to the journalist as she admitted in the article she wrote that evening.

> 'I expected Doris to invite us all to sit in a circle holding hands and watching out for ectoplasm, manifestations and rising tables. But that is not what spiritualism is all about.'

Of course it's not. Little Daniel's ceremony was typical of the ones I perform. There is a written service for the naming ceremony although I rarely follow it. I prefer to be spontaneous but of course there are certain things that one must include. I asked the God-parents to promise to bring Daniel up to believe in the Fatherhood of God and the brotherhood of man, to watch over the child and help the parents wherever possible. Then I offered up a little prayer which goes like this:

Divine Spirit and Creator of all life, and yet very dear Father and Friend of each of us here present, before these witnesses, both seen and unseen, I bring this child to dedicate his life to You and hope You will watch over and guide him.'

Finally I offered up another prayer on behalf of Lynda and her husband Alan, thanking God for allowing them the privilege of becoming parents. Throughout the service Daniel had been a little lamb, there wasn't a peep out of him. Then I placed a bunch of beautiful white freesias against his heart and said, 'I name thee Daniel.' At this stage he stirred. And promptly started to chew the flowers. I said, 'No, darling, give them back to Granny Doris!' That bit doesn't appear in the book of service!

Then we had a champagne buffet lunch to celebrate. The atmosphere in the suite was as bubbly as the champagne, and as I stood in the corner watching the fun I thought back to the scene in the same room only a few hours earlier. There had been no laughter then, as I gave a sitting to a distraught mother trying to discover the truth about her teenage son's tragic death.

Nineteen-year-old Paul Wardle had been found dead

at his home with a plastic bag over his head. The bag had contained glue, but an inquest couldn't decide how the bag had come to be placed over Paul's head, so an open verdict had been recorded.

Mrs Doreen Wardle sobbed as she told me, 'The police say it must have been some sort of experiment Paul was trying out with glue. But he never sniffed the stuff. Please, Doris, please can you help? Can you contact him?'

Paul did come through to us in that room. He mentioned a lot of names that meant nothing to me, but many of them were pals he had written about in his diary. And he told me firmly, 'I wasn't alone, Doris.'

Although he didn't mention how many people were with him, I gained the firm impression there were two or maybe even three. The information was sufficient to reinforce Mrs Wardle's conviction that a new investigation was required.

She later told reporters, 'Doris has told me things that no-one outside the family could have known. She has also given me the strength to fight on until I have unearthed the truth.'

I wish I could have been of more help, but I was pleased to note before I left Liverpool that both a local solicitor and the local Member of Parliament were helping Mrs Wardle in her campaign.

Looking now at those guests laughing and joking at Daniel's party, I thought, 'It's a right old mixture of a day, Doris, girl, and we haven't even got to the Philharmonic Hall yet!'

I could hardly keep my eyes open and I thought to myself: 'Good Lord, wouldn't it be terrible if you dropped asleep in front of the camera.' The gentle rocking motion of the car didn't help either. I kept nodding off and then waking up with a start as we shot round yet another corner. There's not a lot of traffic on the streets at five o'clock in the morning and if I had realized this fact earlier I would have snatched another half hour in bed. As it was I was trying my hardest to appear bright-eyed and wide-awake and wondering how the breakfast time television presenters managed to do it every morning.

It was a Saturday and I had been invited to appear on the ITV programme *Good Morning Britain* with Henry Kelly and a nice young lady called Toni Arthur. Henry and I had met a few years ago on a programme on Irish television and I was looking forward to a good old natter again but I'd never met Toni.

I was particularly happy to be invited to appear on ITV because twelve months earlier a show I had done for Granada had been banned by the Independent Broadcasting Authority twenty-four hours before it was due to be screened. It had led a lot of people to wonder exactly what Doris Stokes did that was so terrifying. So I was now taking every opportunity that presented itself to show people that what I do is the most natural thing in the world – even if it meant getting up before the crack of dawn!

A cup of coffee in the TV AM studios at Camden Lock soon woke me up and then it was into the make-up room where a make-up girl tried her best to make me look as presentable as was possible at this unearthly hour.

Nobody had explained what I was going to do on the show so I tried to relax, which wasn't too difficult, and let whatever wanted to come into my head do just that. I found myself saying to the make-up girl, 'So you live down by the river then?' I don't know what made me say it but the girl almost dropped her powder puff with shock. 'Why yes, Doris, I do. How on earth did you know.' 'I haven't the faintest idea,' I answered honestly. And then the studio manager came in and asked me to follow him to the set.

The first guest on was a kennelmaid with some pedigree dogs and I sat in the wings while she was being interviewed by Henry and Toni. All three of them were deeply engrossed in the conversation. They were so engrossed in fact that nobody noticed what one of the dogs had just done on the studio floor. There was a puddle and it was spreading slowly and silently towards Toni's feet.

I watched in horrified fascination. There was nothing else I could do, after all, the programme was going out live. I could hardly stand up and shout, 'Toni, watch out for that pool!' But even while I was pondering the problem a voice came in my ear and said, 'You've got to warn her somehow.'

Mentally I did my best as Toni got to her feet. And she missed the spot by inches!

'Who are you?' I asked the voice.

'My name is Mrs Hill, I passed over with a stroke.'

Toni was walking backwards now, and somehow she again missed that puddle by a fraction of an inch.

'How do you know Toni?'

'I'm her Nana. But I don't call her Toni . . .'

At that point our conversation ended abruptly. I was due on screen and immediately Toni launched into the questions asking me if I could actually see spirits.

I told her, 'I can see spirit children but that's probably because I'm close to them.' Several other questions followed then Toni said, 'So we've all got somebody looking after us, then?'

161

'Yes,' I said. 'For example, your Nana, Mrs Hill, she came through just now.'

Toni sat bolt upright in surprise. 'You mean my Dad's Mum!' 'Yes,' I continued. 'She came over with a stroke but she says she doesn't call you Toni.'

'No she wouldn't. How incredible. This is giving me goose bumps!'

At that stage Henry Kelly interrupted to ask: 'How do you control it?'

Well of course – as I've explained before – it can be difficult but as I told Henry: 'I have to say push off, darlings. There's a programme on the television I want to watch.' And in fact Henry helped me to control it on this occasion. If he hadn't interrupted we might have got involved in a sitting there and then. And the IBA might have frowned on that.

In fact Henry asked me about the IBA ban and I gave him as honestly as I could the reasons I thought they had prevented the programme from being screened.

'I got too near the bone. A mother whose child I had brought back burst into tears. If I had gone on stage and said in a silly spooky voice "Is there anybody there?" it would have been acceptable.'

Both Toni and Henry nodded in what I think was agreement as I pointed out, 'Nobody laughs all the time and nobody cries all the time. You have rain and sunshine in the weather and you have rain and sunshine in your life. It has to balance out and if it didn't we'd never learn anything at all. It would be an awfully false world if we all went round smiling all the time.'

The rest of our chat went off without a hitch but I was careful not to let it lapse into a sitting because I didn't want to start something we wouldn't be able to finish on air. It wouldn't have been fair to the viewers.

At the same time I was dreading Toni asking me why her Nana had come through. I don't know how I could have told her about the warning. I don't like telling even tiny white lies but I think this is one occasion where I might have had to – or else face a permanent ban from the IBA!

I like to work or be interviewed live on both television and radio because that way everybody knows that what I say is spontaneous and can't be rehearsed. In fact more often than not I don't know what sort of questions I'm going to be asked until we are in the actual studio.

That was the case when I was asked to appear on an afternoon chat show on BBC Radio Nottingham where I was interviewed by a very polite young man called Dennis McCarthey, who began by asking me if I always told the truth.

It was a fair enough question and I told him, 'Yes, I do!'

Even if someone on the other side was unhappy, would you tell their family here?

For the record, and because this is a question I have often been asked, I'll repeat what I told the listeners of BBC Radio Nottingham.

If anyone on the other side is unhappy it is, more often than not, because the loved ones they left behind are unhappy. This can be for a variety of reasons. We all have harsh words to say to the ones we love from time to time, we can't help it, we're human. The real tragedy comes when we've had a row with someone we love and they've died before we can make it up. I've met so many parents whose lives have been torn apart by this happening with their youngsters. They blame themselves every minute of the day and night. They torture themselves with the thought that if there hadn't been a row a tragedy might have been averted. But in every case where I've spoken to these parents and their children have come through, the message has been the same: it is the youngsters on the other side who want to shoulder the blame, or rather point out to their parents that there is no blame to be shouldered on earth. The same sort of guilty feeling comes sometimes when we've lost a loved one and we tell ourselves, 'If only I'd visited them more often. If only I'd spared more of my time.' It's a natural reaction and one that they understand on the other side. But all the grieving and guilt won't bring them back. We have to wait until we are reunited once more on the other side. Meanwhile what is done is done and we must try to live our lives as best we can.

Dennis also asked me if I believed there is a hell and I told him that I don't believe in hellfire as such although there is a bottom plane in the after life that's pretty miserable. In fact I once asked Ramonov: 'You say I must try to lead a good life but what happens when I pass over to the other side? Will I have to mix with the likes of Hitler?'

He told me that the life I lead on this side will determine on what plane I move to on the other side so I live by a very simple rule. Every day I pray, 'Please God, please let me live this day in such a way that I won't be ashamed to face my children if I pass over before the morning.'

Then Dennis said, 'I don't want to do this now because we've come to the end of the programme but if I were to ask you to give me a sitting live on air could you do it?'

Our time was up but already I had received a signal from the spirit world and I watched the look of amazement on his face as I told him, 'I never promise

164

anything but I always say that I will try. In your case I can tell there is someone very special who hasn't been over very long. I can tell because there's a tiny flickering blue light over your shoulder.'

Unfortunately the listeners didn't hear the rest of our conversation but that someone very special did come through to Dennis after the broadcast.

Chapter Sixteen

A biting wind whipped up a discarded newspaper and sent it soaring skywards against the towering walls of the new Concert Hall in Nottingham. Spring had arrived but winter hadn't said its final farewell and there was a distinct nip in the air. As John and I scrambled into the taxi waiting at the stage door we both shivered. It had been a full house with more than 2000 people and the cold air outside contrasted sharply with the warmth of the auditorium.

It was then that I saw the young woman. She was clutching onto her husband's arm in floods of tears. It was too cold to stand around so I said, 'Get in, luv, and tell me. What on earth's the matter?'

She managed to blurt out, 'It's my Mum, Doris, she passed away on Saturday.' And then it was more uncontrollable sobs. Her husband put his arms round her consolingly and looked at me, pleading: 'Is there anything you can do for us please, Doris? She's been like this for the past three days.'

A taxi on a windy night with four people squashed in the back is not really the place to hold a sitting, so I said, 'Look, try not to upset yourself too much. Dry your eyes, give me your number, and I promise I'll ring you in the morning.'

I hadn't even had time to look at that tear-stained piece of paper before the hotel phone rang at nine o'clock the next morning. I didn't need to ask who was calling. A voice in my ear said, 'That'll be my daughter, Doris. You know, the one you spoke to in the taxi last night. She's impatient, couldn't wait for you to phone her.'

I picked up the phone and said, 'Good morning, luv, I thought it might be you calling. I've got your Mum here with me now.'

There was a gasp down the other end of the phone. At least the tears had dried up! The voice in my ear said, 'I'm Maudie, Doris. Tell them I'm with Bill.'

I relayed the message and asked, 'Who is Bill?'

The gasping had now progressed to squeals down the phone. 'It's her Dad, Doris, he died when she was only two but Mum often said she was longing to meet him one day.'

'Tell them not to spend a lot on my funeral, Doris. I'm not in that box, I'm here. Don't let them spend a lot. There's no need for it.' It was Maudie again.

Once again I relayed the message. This time there was a chuckle down the line. 'If that's how Mum wants it, Doris, that's how it will be. God bless you and thank Mum for coming through! I know now I can face the ordeal of the funeral – and I'll manage it without tears. You've proved to me that Mum hasn't really left us at all . . .'

It's that sort of message that makes life as a medium worthwhile. It's nice to be able to get messages through for people who do believe in the spirit world. But when I can prove to others that there is life beyond the earth plane, I'm over the moon. Believing as we do doesn't mean there's no heartache when a loved one passes over – we wouldn't be human if we didn't feel the pain of parting – but there's no despair or desolation because we know that one day we'll be reunited.

It doesn't always take an earth-shattering message to bring proof. How many relatives do we have who've passed over who are really capable of setting the world

167

on fire? That's why I'd like you to read a transcript of a contact typical of the hundreds I made on tour. This one was at Nottingham, but first let me tell you what greeted John and I when we stepped into the dressing-room. There was a long, perspex box containing a dozen beautiful carnations. John picked up a small label lying alongside them and read it out loud: 'With love from Margaret and Arthur Beckinsale.' The message brought tears to my eyes, as lots of happy memories came flooding back.

Margaret and Arthur were the parents of that talented, young actor Richard Beckinsale, star of such television favourites as *Rising Damp* and *Porridge*. His mother had come to me for a sitting after Richard died from a heart attack at the age of 32. I knew that Margaret and Arthur lived in the Nottingham area, but I hadn't seen them since that sitting, although I had heard from Richard's eight-year-old daughter, Katy. The previous year, during one of my stays in hospital, she had cheered me up by sending a poem. It might not have won any great literary award but it was just the tonic I needed at that time. The poem read:

'To Dear Doris,
We hope you will get better
There's not a lot to say
We know you can get better
Tomorrow or today.'

I've always kept that poem close to my heart but, I haven't met either Margaret or Arthur for a couple of years. Looking at those beautiful flowers I guessed they must be in the audience, so there was nothing for it but to go on stage and tell everyone – and ask if the Beckinsales were with us that evening.

They were, of course. 'I'm sure you'd like to acknowledge the lady who gave us all this good-natured lad who made us laugh so often, I said. Margaret stood up to a tremendous ovation and there were tears streaming down her face.

I know she was embarrassed, but I felt it was only right that we should continue to remember someone like Richard who gave so much pleasure to so many people – and to pat his mum on the back too. But no sooner had the applause died down than Richard came through to add his own pennyworth.

'Tell Mum I've been to America with one of the family Doris.'

'Who's been to America recently?' I asked Margaret.'

'My grandson Rupert,' she replied.

'Well Richard says he went too, just to keep an eye on things. And he's also telling me you've been in hospital.'

'True, Doris. I went in for a major operation.'

Richard interrupted, saying, 'No, I mean she's been to hospital for a check-up. Today. And she's all right.'

I duly informed Margaret of the facts – and that she'd also been given a clean bill of health by Richard.

'That's marvellous,' she laughed.

Richard interrupted again saying, 'Let her know, Doris, that I don't feel bitter now. I did at first when I passed over so suddenly. There were so many things I wanted to do. I wanted to be a musician. She knows that. There was no time on the earth plane but it's fine now. I spend a lot of time in the halls of music over here.'

There were tears in Margaret's eyes as I relayed the information. Then Richard told me something that made me hesitate. It concerned his widow, a lovely young actress called Judy Loe. 'I don't know if I should say that,' I said. 'Perhaps your Mum doesn't know.'

'You can tell me anything, Doris. I don't mind,' Margaret said.

So I told her, 'Richard says will you tell Judy he's glad she's found somebody. He says he's pleased for her sake.'

It was obvious Margaret knew what Richard was talking about. The only thing that surprised her was that her son knew too! 'Yes, it's true, Doris, Judy has found a very good friend.'

'Well, Richard says will you pass this message onto her, and will you also please give little Katy a specially big hug from him.'

At that point Richard's voice began to fade. He'd got across the message he wanted to relay. There was a ripple of applause and soon this grew into a crescendo as those lovely people in the audience showed their appreciation of Richard, who had proved even in the after life that he was still as gentle and as caring as ever.

Margaret and Arthur are believers in the after life, but quite a few people in that Nottingham theatre were not. At least, they were not believers when they went into the hall. By the time the evening was over, however, it was a different picture. And throughout the tour I noticed that the majority of contacts were made for people who had had no previous experience or knowledge of the spirit world. Perhaps they had been searching so desperately that the spirit world was using old Doris as a last resort. Whatever the reason, I've been only too pleased to oblige. And we managed to oblige quite a few people that night apart from Margaret and Arthur Beckinsale.

I began by telling the audience that, as usual before

every demonstration, I had spent the afternoon tuning in while sitting in the hotel bedroom.

In fact it had been harder than usual in Nottingham. The central heating had gone on the blink and I'd spent more time waving my arms and trying to keep warm than I had listening to the spirit world.

Even so a number of names had come through to me and I told the audience, 'Before I came out tonight I asked the spirit world to give me a few starters. Now then, do we have anyone here called Davies, June Davies?' A hand shot up in the front row.

'Is there anyone called Speed? Hathaway? And a name that sounds like Scott Alan?' Hands were shooting up all over the place with shouts of 'Over here, Doris,' That's me.' 'That's my Mum.' It was one of the busiest starts to a demonstration I'd ever had. And it pleased me because we were now nearing the end of the tour. I was beginning to feel the strain but it was nice to know my spirit friends were still able and willing to help.

Mr Speed was one of the first people to come to stand in front of the stage and the following is a transcript of what happened:

Doris: Who's John?

Mr Speed: My son.

Doris: I've got a lady's voice coming through and she hasn't been over very long.

Mr Speed: That's right.

Doris: Is John her baby?

Mr Speed: Yes.

Doris: She's telling me, 'Forgive me, Doris, I'm not quite sure what to do.' This is her first contact.

171

It obviously was because when Mr Speed heard this there were tears of emotion running down his cheeks. He nodded and said, 'That's true.'

> *Doris*: She tells me she was in her late fifties and she suffered quite badly.
>
> *Mr Speed*: Yes.
>
> *Doris*: Who's Lily?
>
> *Mr Speed*: Her friend.
>
> *Doris*: She says 'tell Lily I've been back although she won't believe it'. She also tells me she passed over just before an anniversary.
>
> *Mr Speed*: Yes.
>
> *Doris*: She says please don't grieve for her because she did suffer. She'd had enough and just wants you to know she's all right now. She's with Edith. Who is Edith?
>
> *Mr Speed*: That was my mother's name.
>
> *Doris*: She also tells me you've put a photograph of her on the mantlepiece.
>
> *Mr Speed*: That's right, Doris.

There was a bit of humour in the next remark which raised a laugh from the audience when I relayed it, 'She says, "Tell him it's the worse one of the lot!" '

There were still two pieces of evidence I was waiting to hear which I knew would convince Mr Speed. They were the name of the voice that was talking in my ear and the christian name of her husband.

'I'm waiting for you to give it to me, luv. What did you call him?' Again that lovely sense of humour, and more laughter when I gave the reply: 'She says "I know what I'd call him but you'd better call him Harold. That's his name. He's also known as Al." '

172

Harold Speed just said simply: 'That's right, Doris.'

But I still hadn't got his wife's name so I asked again. And she told me impatiently, 'I told you once. I mentioned it. It's Lily.'

There was no point in arguing. In fact she'd mentioned her friend Lily earlier, omitting to tell me that that was her name as well, so I just said out loud, 'Harold, do you believe I've been talking to Lily?'

'Yes I do.'

I said, 'Well if no-one else goes out of here tonight with proof of the spirit world, I'm glad I've done it for you, Harold.'

In front of me now was a young woman – I later discovered her name was Pauline and again, here's a transcript of what happened:

> *Doris*: Your name isn't Scott Alan is it?
> *Pauline*: No
> *Doris*: It's a man's voice I can hear. Your mum, Mrs Scott Alan, is a nurse and this man is connected to her. He went over very quickly.
> *Pauline*: Yes.
> *Doris*: Are you his baby?
> *Pauline*: One of them.
> *Doris*: I can always sense when you belong. I want to come and give you a big hug. He's telling me your mum hasn't been very well. She lives down south and she nurses mentally handicapped people like I used to do.
> *Pauline*: She does, Doris.
> *Doris*: He's saying we have a lot in common. Your Mum writes poetry. He says she gets a lot of inspiration from the spirit world.

173

Pauline: Yes, Doris, she does.

Doris: He tells me she is a very independent woman.

Pauline: Yes she is.

Doris: She's taken one wedding ring off. She has the courage of her convictions. She's prepared to say when things aren't working out.

Pauline: Yes she is.

Doris: He says thanks for looking after her because she's been staying with you. She is also being guided from the other side. Her guide is a nun and it is this nun who inspires her to write the poems. She's to go ahead and have them printed. does that make sense to you?

Pauline: Yes, Doris, it does.

At that point I thought the contact was fading, the man had come out with an enormous amount of detailed information, but he wasn't prepared to disappear just yet.

'Wait a minute, let's make it waterproof for all these people listening,' he said.

I found myself saying: 'Who's Winifred?'

'That's her other name,' came the reply from Pauline.

'Her name is Winifred Jo Scott Alan?'

'That's right!'

Still it hadn't finished. I said: 'They're giving me an address. Somewhere down south.' I came out with the name of a road.

Again Pauline said, 'That's right!' The voice faded. A few days later I received the following letter, addressed to my secretary:

Fareham
Hants

Dear Secretary,

On Tuesday last Doris called my name and address out at a demonstration in Nottingham. I was 200 miles away at my home, my daughter took the message on my behalf.

The evidence given was 100 per cent correct and because of the extraordinary circumstances and my not being in that audience I feel compelled to contact Doris. I so much want her to listen to the enclosed tape as a means of thanks and I have also included my poetry about the mentally handicapped as a small gift.

I understand how busy Doris must be, but can you please ensure that she receives this tape at the earliest possible moment.

Thank you in anticipation,
Nurse Joan Scott Alan

Needless to say, I played that tape as soon as I received it. And I've played it over and over again because it's among the most moving I've ever heard. Listening to it I can tell that nurse Joan Scott Alan is a very special person and she has a wonderful insight into nursing, especially with mentally handicapped people. She also confirmed that she does get help with her work from the spirit world and it came about in a most extraordinary way.

'I don't take any credit for the poems at all,' Joan explained. 'They were spoken to me by an unknown voice in spirit. The titles came to me first while I was working on the wards.

175

'Then the spirit world waited until I was sitting quietly in the nurses' rest room before dictating the first of the poems. At first I had no idea what was happening. I do have a psychic gift and I thought I was being given the names of books to read.

'The same evening, at home, a spirit voice came again and for three hours the poems were dictated to me. I'm so glad my dear old father wants me to publish them. It has been at the back of my mind because it's a way of raising money for our handicapped patients. Now, Doris, you've shown what must be done – and it will be.'

Joan has set her poetry to music and one of the most touching of her collection is about a view of the world as seen through the eyes of a mentally handicapped person. See if you agree with me.

> I watch you move, I hear you talk
> and yet my limbs don't want to walk.
> I move my mouth to let you know
> and yet somehow the words won't flow.
>
>
> I watch your face to test your mood.
> Perhaps you think me very rude
> but I have thoughts and feelings too.
> If only I could talk to you
> to tell you, oh so many things,
> the joy I feel when I hear you sing
> and then, if only I could explain,
> the pains and headaches I contain.
> I shout and rage to make it clear
> but it all falls on stone deaf ears.

Oh dear, here comes that horrid man.
You know, the one who tries to plan
and whispers too
those dreadful things he bids me do.
But you insist he's not there
when all the time he stands and stares.
I try so hard to shut him out.
Why can't you see when he's about?

I want so much to be like you.
To laugh and talk, and play the fool.
To understand and be understood
like everyone in this world should.
But perhaps I'm sent trapped in this frame
to teach mankind a simple game
that love and patience, strength and trust,
you all can learn by helping us.

It makes me feel so humble every time I read that poem.

My visit to Nottingham was almost like a home-coming because I was born in Grantham, which is less than twenty miles away. The man who was chairman for the evening was Derek Hodson who had been a playmate in the dim and distant past and one of my first engagements as a medium, almost forty years ago, had been at the Spiritualist Church in Nottingham. On that occasion there had only been a handful of people, it was slightly different this time. I was in one of the city's biggest halls and it was packed to the rafters. It was nice to see at question time that the majority of people in the queue were youngsters.

It was a question from one of these young people that brought a lump to my throat and made me feel humble. It brought it home to me, that you don't need

177

to be as old as me to have experienced the full pain of living.

Her face was pale and she was trembling as she asked, 'Doris, if a baby dies tragically does he get better on the other side?'

There was tremendous anguish in the voice but there was no need to say any more. A voice was telling me exactly what had happened. She was talking about a toddler who had been violently assaulted and murdered, a child close to her, but not her own.

I said gently, 'Luv, don't worry about that. They've got hospitals on the other side. He'll be nursed back to health with tender loving care. Whatever happened here will be forgotten now and there'll be nothing for him to be frightened of on the other side.'

Then another voice came in my ear. I asked, 'Who's Eileen?'

'That's his mum, Doris.'

Almost at the same time, a voice bubbling with excitement shouted down from the crowded balcony, 'I'm here, Doris, up here! I'm Eileen!'

'I'm glad the voices told me to mention her name. If I hadn't done so I'm quite sure Eileen would have sat with lips clenched throughout the evening. She would have been too overcome with the tragedy that had blighted her life to come down and discuss it with me voluntarily. But the spirit world *had* given me her name. And now her sad eyes were sparkling.

I said, 'Eileen, believe me, nothing will hurt your baby over there. He'll be looked after by a spirit mother, someone young like yourself, or maybe a girl who's never known the joys of motherhood on the earth plane. Whoever he's with he'll be bringing pleasure to them.'

Suddenly a toddler appeared alongside me. He was

178

only about three or four years old and he had fair hair, blue eyes and a beaming smile. He looked down to the front of the stage. The girl who had asked the question was still standing there and there were tears streaming down her face. Then he looked at me with a puzzled look on his face and said, 'What's my auntie crying for, Doris? Please tell her and my Mam that I'm all right. Everything's lovely now.'

Then he said, 'Tell them about Gary please. He used to ride my bike – and he's still got something of mine. And tell Mam, please tell Mam, I saw her get my blue cardigan out and cuddle it.'

Eileen gasped with astonishment as I passed on these messages and described her son. 'It's true, it's true,' she cried. 'Gary was his best friend and he *did* ride his bike!'

Then, just as suddenly as he had appeared, the little mite was gone. The stage was empty again, apart from myself and my old friend Derek Hodson and a huge bunch of yellow chrysanthemums standing on a table between us. I glanced at them and then looked up at Eileen. I said, 'Would you take these home with you, darling, with all our love and with love from your little boy?'

She came down from the balcony, her eyes brimming, and she said: 'Doris, thank you. How did you know? Yellow was his favourite colour.'

There was now so much pleasure in her face that I couldn't stop a lump coming into my throat. I couldn't stop myself, either, from telling everybody what I was feeling. I said: 'Oh Eileen, my luv, please will everybody pray for this mother.'

And as I was saying it, so much more came into my mind. I could picture the little lad picking a bunch of bright yellow dandelions. He would have been

179

attracted to them by the colour. And he would have picked them because the colour would have pleased his Mam.

It's a scene that must have been repeated a million times every spring. Then I thought: How many times does a young child bring in a bunch of brightly coloured weeds from the garden for his mother? And how many times, does a mother say, 'Oh, they really are nice, darling,' and then plonk them on one side? I know it happens because I've done it myself. But we shouldn't. Here was a young Mum whose son would never be able to pick those weeds again and it made me realize yet again that every minute of life is here to be savoured and to be put to use. When a child brings in those weeds from the garden, we should say, 'They really are beautiful, darling,' and then find a jar or a glass to put them in. We should do it because to the child they are beautiful and they were given to us with love. And anything that's given with love is beautiful.

Since my mastectomy a lady has come in to help me clean our flat, and she said to me the first time she arrived, 'My goodness, Doris, don't you have a lot of stuff to dust.'

I apologized and said: 'Yes, luv, I know I have, but I believe that if anything is given to me with love then I mustn't push it away in a cupboard. It goes out on show out of respect, because I know it's been given with feeling. I wouldn't dream of hiding any gift away.'

I know that in the Nottingham Concert Hall that evening everybody joined me in giving the bouquet of flowers to Eileen with love. I could feel that lovely atmosphere as she took them from me. I could feel something else as well. I have always said that once the love link has been forged nothing will ever break

180

it and Eileen's son had proved it yet again. He had come back to offer comfort to his mother and reassure her that he was safe and well. And he'd chosen to come back exactly one year to the night after he had been killed.

Chapter Seventeen

I wasn't in any pain but I couldn't get my breath. I was choking and I could feel myself sinking. I knew exactly what was happening but I couldn't get the words out to explain. Every time I tried to say anything there was a bubbling in my throat and I burst into another fit of coughing. Somehow I managed to look over towards Robin Stephens, another medium who was chairing the meeting, and I gasped, 'I'm sorry, but you'll have to take over for a minute or two, Robin.' Then I staggered to my feet, groped my way through the curtains at the back of the stage and slumped into a chair on the other side. My heart was pounding and my head was swimming.

Just over two hours earlier Robin had introduced me to the audience at the theatre in Camden Town, North London, by saying, 'It's always a delight to listen to other mediums work but especially to Doris Stokes with the conviction that only she seems able to bring to her messages.'

Well, I had to admit there had been plenty of conviction in this latest message which had completely bowled me over. On the other side of the curtain I could now hear a buzz of anxious conversation and then Robin again, calming the situation down. I had just experienced something that had only happened to me once in all my years as a medium. And, as on that occasion, it had happened because I was physically exhausted.

I could hear Robin saying, 'I'm sure that Doris will

182

be quite well again in a few minutes. One of the problems in getting a contact through such as the one she has just received is that sometimes communicators can get very close and on occasions it can adversely affect the medium.'

He was absolutely right. That's exactly what had happened. I had been talking to a young man in the spirit world who had been telling me how he had died. He had been stabbed, murdered and I had experienced his dying seconds.

The contact had begun very quietly about five minutes earlier when a voice came into my ear and said softly, 'I'm Stephen, I'm Stephen.' In fact he spoke so softly I could hardly hear what he was saying. It sounded like 'I was killed on the road,' but I was straining to catch the message. This happens quite often when a spirit is making contact for the first time so I said, 'I can hardly hear you, Stephen, come in closer, luv.'

Then to the audience I said, 'I've got someone here called Stephen. He was killed on the road. I think it might have been some sort of road accident but I don't know yet.'

From halfway down the auditorium a woman shouted to me, 'I've got a Stephen, Doris, and he was killed on the road.' Immediately Stephen's voice came back to me again, much louder and far more urgent. He said, 'That's my Mum, Doris, I *was* killed on the road. I was stabbed to death.'

Stephen moved in so close I could feel him standing alongside me. He said, 'I got it there and there.' And I could feel a slight pressure on my back and my abdomen. 'I nearly didn't go out that night you know, Doris. And the sad thing is that I didn't even start the row. But just tell Mum that everything's all right now.

I don't feel any bitterness. Tell her I've also brought back a rose, she'll know what I mean.'

As he was talking to me I was relaying the messages to his Mum but it was becoming increasingly difficult.

I was choking. I told the audience, 'I'm sorry, I'm sorry. It's bubbling up in my throat.' I started to cough and it was becoming harder to speak. Stephen gave me three names, all men, and I managed to repeat them before staggering off the stage. Stephen must have realized that he hadn't handled his first contact properly, although I couldn't blame the lad. He'd just been over anxious to speak to his Mum and, because I was run down, I'd allowed him to dominate the situation. This had happened to me before, when I was in contact with a man who died from a brain haemorrhage. He also came in too close to me and I suffered his symptoms. I was blind in one eye for a week. Normally I do feel part of the spirit who is speaking to me during sitting, but it happens only for a split second. If I allowed myself to suffer the illnesses of every spirit I contact for any longer than that, life would just become intolerable!

I sat in the armchair behind the stage in Camden Town and thought to myself, 'Doris, girl, you need a rest. This is no good at all.' My breath was coming back, the bouts of coughing had gone, but so, unfortunately, had Stephen. I wasn't unduly worried about this though. He had made his initial contact and I had no doubts he would be back to see his Mum again, although no doubt next time, if he came through me, he'd keep his distance and not be too eager!

At the front of the theatre the audience was drifting away. Robin had explained that I wouldn't be back this evening and there were one or two disappointed faces. Fortunately, Stephen's Mum had been the last contact of the evening so I was pleased we hadn't let anyone else down, but I would have liked to have completed his message for her.

I needn't have concerned myself about that. His Mum spoke to a journalist who was in the audience after I had left the stage. This is what she said:

> 'The names Doris gave were those of Stephen's father, another relative and the man who killed Stephen. We were all out together having a meal. There was a row, just as Doris described, but it wasn't Stephen's fault. He was trying to intervene and prevent trouble.
>
> 'The horror of that evening is still a vivid and shocking memory, or at least it was until this evening. But now Stephen has come through and spoken to me it will be easier to live with.
>
> 'I'm pleased about the red rose. It shows Stephen still takes an interest in what we do. I visit his grave every month and each time I put one red rose on it.'

I was back in my flat with my feet up. We were now nearing the end of the tour and somebody had worked out that more than 100,000 people had spent *An Evening With Doris Stokes*. And that's not counting the spirit people who came along! On top of that, there were countless radio broadcasts up and down the country, newspaper interviews and television appearances which meant that our message had gone out to many times the number of people who had come to the theatres.

John was doing the housework and the shopping and our son, Terry, was now a dab hand at preparing a whole variety of meals. And I felt as if I could sleep for a whole month! There was no chance of that of course, certainly not until the tour was over. So I decided to compromise. I spent three days resting indoors catching up on letters that pour in every week. And reading through them was probably one of the greatest tonics I could possibly have wished for.

I had noticed since the beginning of the tour the increasing number of young people who were not only coming to see me but also writing some of the most beautiful letters. My Dad used to say to me, 'Cast your bread on the water with love, Doll, and it'll always come back buttered!' And I know exactly what he meant. Sifting through my mail always makes me realize what a wonderful opportunity God has given me to help other people. Just read this youngster's letter and you'll see what I mean:

Wokingham,
Berkshire.

Dear Mrs Stokes,

I am writing to tell you how much I enjoyed your books. It cheered me up to know that people who die are going somewhere much better than this earth.

Recently four people I have known have died, but until their deaths and reading your books I had not really considered spirits in depth, although I have always believed something is there.

By reading your books my fear of dying has decreased and in one way I'm glad those four people, including my Grandad, have passed on. I know they've not said goodbye to us but are waiting and one day we'll all be in eternal life together.

Thank you and keep up your good work.

Yours faithfully,
Carol Prince (aged fifteen)

It's that sort of letter that acts as a better pick-me-up than anything the doctor could have ordered. But, of course, it isn't just the letters from the youngsters that perk me up. Here's another that arrived in the same postbag but from someone a little bit older.

Spinney Hill
Northampton

Dear Doris,

I would like to thank you for the help you have given me through your books.

On New Year's Day last year, my twenty-year-old son David died in a motorcycle accident. He was such a sparkling, lively boy, always laughing and full of fun. He was like a ray of sunshine and the day he died the sun stopped shining for me. That was before I read your books and I can only say now that my prayers have been answered. God bless you and thank you once again.

Mrs J Walters

Mrs Walters also sent me a poem that somebody gave to her shortly after her son died. I've received the same poem from several other people but nobody seems to know who wrote it. I'd like you to read it because it really is one of the most beautiful pieces I've ever read and it's got a special place reserved in the corner of my flat I've devoted to my spirit children.

187

I'll lend you for a little while a child of mine, God said,

For you to love the while he lives, and mourn for when he's dead.

It may be six or seven years, or forty-two or three,

But will you, till I call him back, take care of him for me?

He'll bring his charms to gladden you. And should his stay be brief

you'll always have his memories as a solace in your grief.

I cannot promise he will stay, since all from earth return,

But there are lessons taught below I want this child to learn.

I've looked this whole world over in my search for teachers true

and from the folk that crowd Life's lane I have chosen you.

Now will you give him all your love and not think the labour vain,

nor hate me when I come to take this lent child back again?

I fancy that I heard them say 'Dear God, Thy will be done.

For all the joys this child will bring the risk of grief we'll run.

We will shelter him with tenderness, we'll love him while we may

and for all the happiness we've ever known, we'll ever grateful stay.

But should the angels call him much sooner than we'd planned we will brave the bitter grief that comes, and try to understand.'

Isn't it beautiful? And I know from the letters I've received with those verses slipped inside that it has brought comfort to a great many people. I do really love poetry and another piece which arrived in my postbag was this one:

Love

I looked for Love, and there it was – in the innocent eyes of a child
I looked again and there it was – in a creature shy and wild.
Again I looked, and lo! I saw a fluffy cloud float by
Rosy-rimmed with sunset rays in a beautiful azure sky.
The sparkling sea reflected Love – I thought my heart would burst
As Love began to flow within and quenched my aching thirst;
For I had sought this Love so long, so hard, in many a diverse way
Sat and thought, walked and talked, and often knelt to pray;
Yet when the flood-gates opened up and the river burst its dam
I saw that Love was everywhere – and in everything – for Man.
I had looked outside without success and tried to look within,
As each day passed I must confess my patience wore quite thin,

Until one day I ceased to strive, and began to live each
day –
Each day brought forth a glowing gem which helped
to light the way
To the secret sought by Man – my heart had found the
key –
'Tis Love – so simple – yet 'tis all – to know Eternity.

Sue Coad

The letters about relatives and friends really touch
my heart and it's ones like this which make me realize
there's no point at all in trying to put on airs and
graces. Just be yourself.

Brighton

Dear Doris,

I have been drawn towards spiritualism these
past few months and several mediums have told
me I should join a circle because I'm very psychic.

All these messages sounded wonderful to me. I
thought how purposeful one's life would be if one
could do all this, but then I had second thoughts.
Why on earth would the spirits want me? I'm far
from perfect! I get angry now and again and
sometimes I swear, although I try not to do it too
often. I get unpleasant thoughts about some people
though I would like to like everybody, but I find
it impossible and I try to work out why.

So, when I read your story with you openly
telling of your own human weaknesses I realized
that we are not, after all, expected to be perfect.
How can we be? We wouldn't be here if we were!

I'm now starting to learn and, although I know you don't regard yourself as a great philosopher, I'd like you to know you have played an important part in my progression.

With love from
Linda Sinclair

Isn't that nice? But honestly it's Linda who has helped herself to progress by simply accepting that she is an ordinary human being and not a saint. None of us are.

I'll end this selection from our postbag with two beautiful poems. And I hope you'll be able to see why reading through my mail is the best tonic in the world.

To Mrs Doris Stokes and John Michael

The day will come when I will stand
At the entrance to that perfect land.
And there to greet me will be my son
Who will gently show me those wonders to come
In that place where sunshine never ends.
Where the shining waters flow
Through hills and valleys evergreen
Bathed in a golden glow.
And in those heavenly halls I'll find
The love and beauty that will always be mine.
And once again a mother I'll be
To that son I loved so tenderly.

B.W.

For Doris,

For all the little Children
You were awoken from your sleep.
The Light chose you to champion
the little one's beliefs
They come to you in hundreds,
they know you to be true;
They tell you all their secrets
They know that you will keep,
and when they bring their families,
they know you'll ease their grief.
What an honour to be chosen,
Your work is very hard,
But they knew that when they chose you
they had picked the best by far.
If I could give one tiny part
of me to help you through,
Then it would be my loving heart,
to match your own so true.

Dianne Jones,
Doncaster.

May I just say thank you to both of you and bless you
for such beautiful words.

Chapter Eighteen

'How can my daughter know about things that happened before she was born?' This was the first time the question had been asked on tour and behind it lay fascinating proof of the psychic powers of children.

I was back in the Wythenshawe Forum, Manchester again and half a world away from the Falklands. And yet, as soon as the question was asked, my mind turned to the chaos and carnage of that tragic war. It was so vivid that I could smell the smoke and hear the frantic warnings screamed above the crackle of gunfire and the shrieking of jet engines.

It was so far from this cosy theatre and the link lay in two names that came into my ear. Lindsay and Steven. I said to the woman standing in front of me, 'Is your daughter called Lindsay?' She couldn't disguise the surprise in her voice as she replied, 'Good Lord, yes she is, Doris.'

'And you had a son – Steven?'

'He was killed in the Falklands, Doris.'

At that moment he strolled on stage with a broad grin on his face, so I said, 'He hasn't left you, luv. He's here with me now. He's sending his love to you and to Lindsay.'

And that solved the mystery of how Lindsay knew about things that happened before she was born. She was having regular chats with her big brother. In fact the little girl had told her mum this and Mrs Ann McNeil had just wanted confirmation from me.

Steven McAndrew was Ann's son by a previous

marriage and when his father died Ann had married again. Lindsay was in fact his step-sister but she hero-worshipped her big brother.

And big brother was a lad with a thirst for adventure. He signed up with the Royal Marines and was at the forefront of the battle for San Carlos on the Falklands. He had been a machine-gunner. The screaming of a jet engine I had heard had been an Argentinian Skyhawk which dropped a 500lb bomb on his trench.

Steven had been fighting to the very end but he told me, 'I didn't feel a thing, Doris, so please tell the family not to upset themselves. We'll meet again.' There was no bitterness in his voice and certainly his visits to his little sister didn't frighten her, as Ann explained later.

'Steven and Lindsay were as close as any brother and sister could be, despite the difference in their ages. Steven looked after her a lot and after he was killed Lindsay moved into his bedroom. She cried a lot when I first broke the news to her that he wouldn't be coming home and then she cheered up and began telling us how she talked to Steven.

'At first, my husband and I took no notice. It was the sort of thing any mother would expect from a little girl who had lost the brother she loved. I thought she was just inventing it to soften the blow to herself.'

But six weeks after Steven's death came the proof that Lindsay was not inventing her conversations. She jumped into bed with her mum and dad and said, 'Steven's in heaven with Graham and Elsa. He's told me.'

The message shook Ann and her husband Tony

rigid. She said, 'Lindsay knew about my first husband, whose name was Graham, but she couldn't have known that he had a dog. And that the dog was called Elsa.'

Three months later came further evidence of Steven's visits to his little sister. The McNeil family were staying at a holiday camp when Lindsay said, 'Steven's been telling me how he cut his chin when he slipped on a bar of soap at school.'

It was something his mum had completely forgotten about. It was absolutely true, but something that little Lindsay could not have possibly known. It wasn't long after this incident that Steven made a brief appearance to his mum – in a dream.

'I felt he was pulling me out of bed, telling me the lounge was on fire. It was such a realistic dream that it woke me up and I went downstairs to check that everything was all right. There was a smouldering cigarette in a waste paper basket just catching alight.'

Steven was still watching over his family and I was pleased he popped in when his mum came to see me at the Wythenshawe Forum. Steven asked me to give her the big bunch of flowers that the management of the theatre had put on stage for me. I was happy to oblige, of course, but there was a little sequel to this story which I'll leave to Ann.

'When I got home after seeing Doris, Lindsay was standing in her nightie at the top of the stairs. She was rubbing her eyes and had obviously just got up out of bed.

'I said "What are you doing up, young lady?" She replied, "You haven't shown me the flowers the lady gave you."

'I was stunned, but before I could say anything

Lindsay added, "Steven's told me about them. And he says he liked that lady." '

Now that's the first time I've ever been paid a compliment by the spirit world! And I'm pleased to say that when I last heard from Ann, Steven was still visiting his little sister occasionally. I was also pleased to hear that Ann doesn't allow anyone else to question her about it and, if she mentions Steven, the family treat it as a normal and natural occurrence. And it is for children.

Chapter Nineteen

The carpet was so deep it almost came over my ankles. Or, at least, that's the way it felt. And the chandeliers were like those that you only see in films. They were magnificent. It really was a fairytale setting and all round John and me were lots of famous faces, most of whom we'd only seen on the television before. But it was terribly hot and there was only champagne to drink. Unfortunately, I have to admit I don't have the taste for it and neither does John. Standing there, in the middle of one of the poshest hotels in London, we would have given anything for a cup of tea.

We were guests at the annual lunch of *Woman's Own* magazine, and I'd been flabbergasted when the editor's secretary telephoned me to say: 'We're inviting a number of women whose achievements over the past year we should like acknowledged. We'd like you to come Mrs Stokes.'

I could hardly believe my ears. A woman of achievement! I must admit I was more than a bit chuffed and I accepted straightaway, although for the life of me I really felt that there were far more deserving people around. Whatever I had achieved was done with God's help, it was a team effort. I'd hardly climbed Mount Everest or sailed round the world single handed, but if *Woman's Own* thought that I deserved the honour of being asked somehow, one way or the other, I was going to prove worthy of the invitation. At this stage I hadn't the faintest idea how or what I could do, but I knew my spirit friends would not let me down, they would give me guidance – and they did of course by allowing me the privilege of raising money for the Save the Children Fund charity which *Woman's Own* were supporting.

There was an added bonus as the magazine was also launching an appeal to build a Bone Marrow Unit and Princess Anne, as President of the Save the Children Fund, was coming to the lunch as guest of honour. I am constantly amazed that in this day and age, when we can send people to the moon, we still can't raise enough money to buy equipment to stop sick children from dying. It breaks my heart sometimes and I wonder what's happened to our priorities. During the past year, however, I have done what I can to boost that bone marrow unit fund.

Princess Anne looked a picture, so beautiful, with her soft fair hair swept off her face in a regal style and her ice blue dress fitting her tiny figure so perfectly. I couldn't help thinking how small and frail she looked and yet so strong and determined when fighting for something which she believes is right. Here's someone, I thought, who really is a woman of achievement. Here's a real live princess who doesn't just sit back in the lap of luxury. She's a worker like the rest of us and what's more important is that she cares what happens to the human race. If anyone deserved to be at that lunch Her Royal Highness Princess Anne did.

John and I were lined up with everyone else waiting to be presented to Princess Anne, the excitement mounting as the big moment drew nearer. But as the tension rose so did the temperature of the place and there wasn't a cup of tea in sight. I could see that John was going a bit green round the gills, too, so I said, 'Look, luv, we'll have to find somewhere cooler and get a drink of water or something or else we're both going to faint.' He agreed so we both set off in search of a loo and the hotel being the size it was, that took some time. But that first sip of water was more refreshing than a magnum of champagne on ice. I remember looking at the gilt mirrors on the wall of that powder room and thinking back to the delights of drinking water as a child back home in Grantham. Mother used to keep a pail of it on a stone slab in the pantry during hot weather. Dipping into that clear ice cold water when you were all hot and bothered was one of life's great luxuries.

I grinned to myself and thought, 'Did you ever imagine, Doris, you'd one day be drinking water in such splendid surroundings?'

But I never did get to meet Her Royal Highness. By the time John and I found our way back again, the presentations were over and everyone was sitting down to their meal!

I might have missed Princess Anne but there were compensations. Sitting at our table was someone who has become a great friend since that day. He's a wonderfully genuine person with a great sense of humour and a warm personality, although most of the time he's in disguise so you'd never know. He's Danny la Rue. And from the moment we met we got on like a house on fire.

He greeted me like a long-lost friend and gave me a big hug. I can't pretend that I wasn't flattered that he knew my name and for a second or two I felt a bit tongue-tied, but Danny's easy-going manner and the way he was so obviously interested in hearing what I had to say soon put me at my ease. And I found I had plenty to say after Danny told me he had given away all his mother's possessions since her death.

Almost without thinking about what I was saying,

I replied: 'No you haven't. Not everything. There's still a cameo. It's in some sort of envelope or bag and it's kept in a drawer.'

Danny looked at me in surprise. Then he said, 'Good lord! You're right, Doris. I've kept it because it was the last thing I bought her and I'd never part with it.'

It was sometime later that Danny's manager told me that he looked after it and kept it in an office drawer. And Danny admitted, 'I put it in a Marks and Spencer bag, Doris, for safekeeping!'

The next time Danny and I met was in Birmingham. I was at the Odeon for two nights and he was appearing in a pre-London run of the musical *Hello Dolly*. John and I had just settled into our hotel room when the phone rang and a voice said, 'Hello, Doris. It's Danny. Welcome to Birmingham and what about a cup of tea?' He'd remembered that I didn't like champagne. Within a couple of hours we'd got the cups out and settled down for a chat. Almost immediately we were joined by Danny's mum. And she'd brought along his father Patrick for good measure. She told me her name was Mary Anne, which Danny confirmed, and then said that her son's full name was Daniel Patrick Carroll – which Danny again confirmed.

But then Mary Anne's voice took on an anxious tone and, after listening to what she said, I asked Danny, 'How do you get on with the rest of the cast? Do you trust everybody?'

He seemed surprised at the question but answered without hesitation: 'They're a marvellous crowd, Doris, and I'd trust them all with my life. We're all one big happy family.'

I said: 'Well, I have to tell you that your Mum's

200

worried about something. I get the impression that she thinks somebody there is jealous of you and will try to do something that will harm the show, so please be careful.'

The information didn't seem to worry Danny too much, and it certainly didn't put him off his tea. We chatted on for at least another hour until it was time for him to get ready for his own show. 'I'll see you soon,' he said as he rushed out of the door. And he did see me soon. In fact it was much sooner than I expected. Three hours later, after his own show had finished, Danny raced round to the Odeon to make a surprise appearance alongside me on the stage.

The audience loved it. And, of course, they insisted that he sang for them. So the *Evening With Doris Stokes* ended with Danny and me singing *On Mother Kelly's Doorstep* together and everybody else joining in. It was a lovely way to end a demonstration and it also showed what a truly great artiste Danny is. I felt so proud that a big star like him could take the time to come along to join me and my friends.

Unfortunately though, Mary Anne was right about that spot of bother, although it had nothing to do with the cast of his show, for a few days later somebody stole the musical score to *Hello Dolly*. It took a lot of extra time and trouble to replace it but, despite the hiccough, the show did open on time – and Danny invited John and I along to the West End to see it.

Actually that meeting with Danny led to two other nice things happening. I met Bert Weedon who wrote some beautiful music for a long-playing record I made and we had a visit from my old friend Dick Emery, by now in the spirit world.

The meeting with Bert came when the promoters who were handling my tour decided there ought to be a permanent record of it in the form of an LP. One side of the record would be recorded from some of the demonstrations and on the other I'd talk to my friend Nancy about spiritualism. It sounded a good idea but I felt it needed just a little bit more. I wasn't sure what because I've never been involved in making records or anything like that before. I just knew something was missing. I was still puzzling over it the night John and I went to see *Hello Dolly*.

I didn't know at the time but Bert Weedon is also a spiritualist. And a friend of Danny la Rue. Danny had phoned him earlier that day and said, 'You've said you'd like to meet Doris, so why not come along to the theatre tonight?' And there he was when I walked into Danny's dressing-room after the show. Bert plays the sort of music I like and I've always been an admirer of his, but I never thought we'd actually meet one day. I was over the moon. For a man with so much talent he was remarkably modest. In fact, it was because he was so natural and understanding that I plucked up the courage to talk to him about the record. 'Doris,' he told me, 'I'd like to help. What you need is some music and I'd be happy to write and arrange it for you.'

And that was how, almost forty years after the spirit world gave it to me, the poem about John Michael was set to music. The music Bert wrote for it was as haunting as the words themselves. I know that countless people have shared the comfort that the poem brings and I hope that now even more people will get pleasure from the music that goes with it. I never get tired of reciting John Michael's poem. I've repeated the words a million times and they still bring a lump to my throat. If it's the first time you've read it then I hope it brings you as much pleasure as it has me.

In a baby castle just beyond my eye
My baby plays with angel toys that
   money cannot buy.
Who am I to wish him back
Into this world of strife?
No, play on my baby,
You have eternal life.

At night when all is silent
And sleep forsakes my eyes
I'll hear his tiny footsteps come
   running to my side.
His little hands caress me so
   tenderly and sweet
I'll breathe a prayer and close my
   eyes
and embrace him in my sleep.

Now I have a treasure
that I rate above all other,
I have known true glory –
I am still his mother.

I didn't know at the time but Bert had also read the poem before we met and even then he had wanted to put the words to music. When he came round to our flat, guitar under his arm and arrangement in his pocket, I didn't know what to expect. But as soon as he played the first note tears came into my eyes. The music was inspired. There was no doubt about that in my mind. And by the time Bert had finished the piece I was weeping buckets.

As the last note faded away, a voice in my ear said, 'That was nice, wasn't it, girl? You'll be all right with Bert, he's a good lad you know.' I recognized the voice instantly. We had become mates before he passed over.

In fact he had visited me on one of my many stays in hospital.

I thought: 'What on earth's he here for?' And out loud I said, 'Tell me, Bert, did you know Dick Emery by any chance?'

'Yes, Doris, I did. Why do you ask?'

'Well,' I said. 'He's just put the seal of approval on that music. He likes it as much as I do!'

I thought it was nice of Dick to pop in and offer his advice, and it reminded me of the times when he was alive and would ask my advice – although he very rarely took it. I think he was just looking for a shoulder to cry on. He was a very sad character deep down and every time I saw Dick clowning on television I used to think, 'Why is it that someone who can bring so much happiness to others can't find true happiness himself?'

It is a fact, though, that quite often where there's a lot of talent there is also a lot of self-torment. Tommy Cooper was another man who was highly intelligent and used to work himself up into a terrible state just to make other people happy. The night he died John and I were watching his show on television. I saw him collapse and then almost immediately I saw his spirit body rise up and hover a few feet above the stage. I said to John, 'Oh my God, luv, he's passing over.' And, of course, that's what happened.

A week after that incident a strange thing happened when John and I were staying at the Holiday Inn, Leicester. We had been booked into a magnificent suite. But despite the plush surroundings I didn't have a particularly good night's sleep because one of the doors kept opening and closing. Then I heard Tommy Cooper's voice. He was giving that old familiar laugh of his and saying, 'Nice bed that, Doris, ha, ha. I slept there you know. Ha ha! I can open the door you know.

204

Just like that.' And the door opened itself again. I got up to close it once more and decided to make myself a cup of tea.

The kettle was standing on a sort of breakfast bar in the suite lounge. Next to it I noticed there was a visitor's book. Casually I opened it and started reading the names. There were pop stars, footballers and a lot of names that meant nothing to me at all. Then, across one page was scrawled a name that made my tummy turn over. It was Tommy Cooper's! The kettle boiled and I made myself that cuppa. Then, before I climbed back into bed, I got my own pen out of my handbag. In the visitor's book I wrote, 'This one is for you dearest Tommy. God bless you and God bless all the people who look after you.'

It might have been my imagination but as I pulled the sheet up over me I could have sworn I heard just one final chuckle. And then I fell soundly asleep.

Another passing that saddened me terribly while I was on tour was that of Diana Dors. I was sad because she had been such an inspiration to other people with her courageous fight against cancer. Like myself, she had beaten it more than once and wasn't afraid to talk about it. We were in Stoke-on-Trent when John and I heard she had been taken back into hospital and one of my biggest regrets is that I wasn't able to see her before she passed over.

Diana and Pat Seed, another marvellous woman who has battled for years against cancer, raising a million pounds for a scanner in the process, had become great friends of mine. We used to phone each other to offer mutual consolation when we were feeling low. On other occasions we'd just ring each other up to have a good laugh. I'm afraid we could be rather disrespectful at times and just a little bit rude. We had a little club which we called the 'Sod it' club. That's what we thought about cancer and we all agreed the only way to beat it was to laugh at the disease.

Before my last little do in hospital I rang Diana for a bit of moral support. She raised my spirits enormously and I marched into the ward with our club's slogan ringing in my ears. But, looking back, I get a bit angry with myself for being so self-centred. As it happened I was only suffering from a trapped nerve which the doctors cured. Even when I spoke to Di, moaning like an old woman, she knew that she too had to go back into hospital suffering from a recurrence of cancer. She had postponed it because she wanted to finish a film she was making. But she never let on to me. That heart of gold wouldn't allow her to burden me with her problems.

Instead she let me grumble on while she offered a sympathetic ear, without a hint of the torment she must have been suffering. She was a totally unselfish person and a fighter to the end and I know that Di's husband, Alan Lake, was devastated when she passed over. They were so much in love and perfect for each other.

On the morning of Di's funeral I woke up at about six o'clock with a voice whispering in my ear. It said, 'You know, Doris, I'm glad in a way they dressed me up but please tell that husband of mine that it isn't me in the coffin. That's only an old shell. Tell him I'm still close to him, only a whisper away, and I still love him dearly. Tell him also that Minnie met me when I came over.' I duly relayed the information and discovered that Minnie was Alan Lake's mother. Later that day Alan laid a wreath on Di's coffin with the inscription, 'I love you. You're only a whisper away.'

Chapter Twenty

The lift was shooting up like a rocket and I felt as if I had left my tummy on the ground 600 feet below. But I was thankful for small mercies. At least I was sitting down, perched on a small stool in the corner. I glanced up at John and my friend Nancy. John was swaying from side to side and staring blankly in front of him. Nancy's eyes were shut tight and she was clenching her teeth. It was terrifying and there was worse to come.

We were on our way to the top of London's Telecom Tower where I was to conduct a psychic experiment with readers of a national newspaper. When I'd first been asked to help I jumped at the chance. I am a firm believer that it's possible to transfer messages by thought. After all, that's the way the spirit world contacts most of us. But when the newspaper representatives told me exactly where they wanted me to carry out this experiment, I began to have some thoughts of my own about the idea. On the other hand, I had agreed to do it, so there was nothing for it but to go ahead, taking John and Nancy with me for moral support.

So here we were speeding upwards so fast I felt as if we were on our way to the moon. And not for the first time in the past twelve months I thought, 'Stokes, what are you doing? You must be mad!' The lift seemed to take ages to climb to the top of the 620-feet-high tower but it couldn't have been more than a minute or so and when it finally stopped three very wobbly characters emerged. I don't like heights at the best of times and the lift had brought us to the floor which used to be the restaurant. It's been closed for some years, since the IRA bomb explosion, but there is still a magnificent panoramic view of London. Magnificent, that is, if you like heights, and none of us did.

In fact, we stood as close to the centre of that circular room as we could. You could almost hear our knees knocking. Then the newspaper photographer who had travelled up with us said, 'Come on, Doris. Let's have a picture of you leaning up against the window looking out over London!' I was speechless with fright. I couldn't move! Eventually I managed to splutter, 'You're having a joke, of course, aren't you? Aren't you?' But I could tell by the look on his face he wasn't. Somehow I managed to edge myself towards the open window. I still don't know how I did it. I stood there waiting. There was a pause and the photographer said, 'You'll have to open your eyes, luv. I can't take a picture of you looking like that!'

It seemed the worst two minutes of my life but somehow I managed to satisfy the cameraman and then we got on with the experiment.

I was given three big cards and on each of them was a diagram. The first showed the sun, the second was a silhouette of a house and the third was a water sign showing three wavy lines. At exactly midday I had to concentrate hard on the first symbol and pass my hands over it, and then do the same with the other symbols at two-minute intervals. The newspaper's readers had been asked to tune in at exactly the same time and put down what they thought the symbols looked like. Six minutes later I told the photographer, 'It's worked. I can feel it. The experiment has been a success.' And I could feel it. As I was concentrating on those symbols there was a tremendous vibration in the air. I could almost reach out and touch it. In fact the atmosphere was so good I'd completely forgotten about my fear of heights. Even so, I didn't go back near the window again.

A week later the results were announced. The newspaper told its four million readers it had proved a mind-bending success! Out of the huge response, almost one-third of the people taking part had picked up at least one of the drawings. Even more startling was the number of people who actually got all three of them right. And some people were able to describe in words exactly what they saw.

The paper called in one of Britain's leading statisticians, those experts on facts and figures. And she said, 'Statistically the results are amazing.' In fact I didn't regard them as amazing at all because I know that most of us do have some psychic power and I took part in this experiment to prove it.

What I find amazing is that other people, like the statistician, who's got more brains than I'll ever have, should find something so normal and natural as psychic power uncanny. All it needs to bring it out is faith and lots of love.

Once again my feet were sinking into a carpet that was coming over my ankles. And, once again, I felt distinctly uncomfortable. But this time I wasn't in a posh hotel. I was in a dressing-room and about to go on stage in front of one of the biggest audiences of the tour. I was at the Dominion Theatre in Tottenham Court Road, London. I felt my heart would burst with pride: my name in lights at a West End theatre. And I'd been given the star dressing-room. What on earth was my dad thinking watching me now? He had been a true psychic but I'm sure even he could never have visualized anything like this. And six years ago neither could I.

I sat in a huge armchair and thought, 'It's a good job we can't see into the future.' I'm sure if we could, half of us, including myself, would feel like giving up the ghost straight away! But I wonder if some of us have unconscious premonitions of the future? I was pondering over this because of a sitting I had held a week earlier.

I'd received a phone call from a professional gentleman who lives in the north of England. His wife had died tragically and he wanted to visit me with his two daughters. One of them was a bit dubious about mediums and the afterlife and, on the motorway travelling to London, she said to her father, 'There's one thing very personal that only Mummy and I knew about Daddy. If this lady mentions it, then I'll know Mummy has really spoken to us.'

I've promised not to reveal the name of that family but I can tell you that during a two-hour sitting their mother did come through. And she supplied the proof her daughter was looking for. Before they left, the family gave me a copy of the funeral service which contained a poem their mum had written two years before her tragic death.

As I sat in that dressing-room, waiting to go on stage at the Dominion, I read the poem again.

To My Family

Time is the great healer
All that is past is passed
There are many things in life
We must experience so that

210

We can step forward in spirit.
It takes time to know this,
The Dawn has to come,
Light to enlighten, rising like a
Bird from the Gloom, to fill the eyes,
the senses, the feelings
With bright glimmering understanding.
Dawn may last a thousand years.
But it is already filling the Universe.
Everyone should seek the Dawn,
and so be born again.

This lady certainly knew deep down that there was a life somewhere which was much better than the one here on earth. I could also feel she was a warm person who cared for other people and every time I read that poem it brings me comfort, as it was doing then. Suddenly, a hidden loudspeaker in that posh dressing-room burst into life and I jumped about a foot in the air. I had been miles away but I immediately recognized the voice. It was Tony Ortzen, the editor of *Psychic News* and chairman for the evening.

He was already on stage and I heard him telling the audience, 'I've known Doris now for about ten or twelve years and I'd like to pay her what at first may sound a strange compliment. This can best be done by giving you an everyday example. If you or I were standing at a supermarket check-out and saw her we'd just think she was somebody's mum getting the shopping. That's because Doris is a very ordinary person with an extraordinary gift.'

He was making me blush. I get really embarrassed when people say things like that, especially when I've then got to go out on the stage. I looked at the poem again and I thought, 'Lots of people have extraordinary

211

gifts if only they knew how to use them. The lady who wrote this certainly had a wonderful gift and she was using it, perhaps without fully realizing what she was doing.'

Then, for the umpteenth time in the past twelve months, my knees started knocking and my mouth went dry. Even after all the places we'd visited on the tour, I still got stage fright. I still wondered if the spirit world would make contact or if they would let me down. It never has, of course, but that never stops me worrying. That night the trembling in my bones was worse than ever. This was one of the biggest theatres I'd ever been in.

I breathed in deeply and hoisted myself out of the chair, putting the poem back in my handbag. As I walked down to the wings I thought about the thousands of new friends John and I had made on the tour. I thanked God for giving me the strength to have completed so many miles and for letting me help so many people.

There had been times when I didn't think my health was going to stand up to it all. I thought back to what my guide Ramonov had said to me on the one occasion when I had asked when my time would come to pass over. He had said there was still much to be done and he was right. There still is much to be done. And please God my strength will hold out for some time to come so I can keep doing it.

I was now standing by the curtains and took another deep breath before walking out onto the stage.

At first I couldn't see a thing; the lights were blinding me. But I felt the warmth of the applause as wave after wave of it swept up towards us. It was a lovely sensation.

'How many of you have never been to a demonstration before?' I asked. Most of the hands in the audience went into the air.

'Well, don't expect ghostly voices or spooks walking through walls. There's nothing like that. In fact, there's nothing to be frightened of at all. It's only Doris.'

Chapter Twenty-One

It seems like only yesterday that I fell head over heels in love with Sergeant John Fisher Stokes. Actually stumbled is a better word because that's exactly what happened. I tripped over his feet in a pub. We were married within a week. I can still remember waiting for him in that shop doorway next to Grantham Register Office one cold January morning during the dark days of the last war.

We may have had our love to keep us warm, but like so many young couples we were both in the Forces and terrified of losing each other, living each day we spent together as though it was our last and thanking God each morning for another day of reprieve. And of course when my paratrooper husband was posted missing at Arnhem I really did think our marriage was over. I lost all hope of ever seeing him again. During those bleak sad days never in my wildest dreams could I have imagined that forty years later we'd be sitting in our own flat planning how we would spend our ruby wedding day. We'd never had a proper wedding reception, in the days of rationing they were few and far between, we were happy with just a pot of tea and a bite to eat at the home of the couple who had acted as witnesses for us. It was all we could afford or even expected. We were madly in love and a great big spread with lots of guests was really the last thing we wanted. We had each other and that was enough.

Over the years though, John and I have made friends

in all walks of life, in all parts of the country, in fact all over the world and if I have any regrets looking back over our time together it's only that it has been impossible for us to keep in regular contact with everyone. We've done our best and so have our friends, even if it has only meant a hastily scribbled note once a year on the back of a Christmas card. My thoughts had turned to absent friends on the day of our ruby wedding. Terry had promised to take us out for dinner and I was looking forward to it. We wanted nothing posh and Terry had insisted that he arrange everything and reluctantly I had agreed although I was thinking to myself how nice it would be to contact one or two old friends and ask them to celebrate with us. But Terry was adamant that it was his treat and we had to leave all the arrangements to him. He tried to give the impression that there would be nothing really special, although I haven't been his mother for more than thirty years for nothing – and I suspected something was afoot.

Weeks before our anniversary Terry had been making furtive phone calls and disappearing for hours at a time. If I caught him on the telephone the conversation would stop abruptly or he'd start talking about the weather. In fact it got to the stage when I was so curious to know just what was going on that I'd half a mind to call in Ramonov! Eventually I convinced myself that Terry was having a cake made for us with forty candles and it would be ceremoniously brought in over our dinner.

John came to the same conclusion and neither of us gave it much more thought, which is probably just as well because I don't think by any stretch of the imagination we could truly have expected or imagined what our son Terry had laid on for us.

There was indeed a cake with forty candles but the setting was in one of the most luxurious suites in a hotel in the West End of London. And there weren't just one or two old friends but more than a hundred of them who had travelled from Land's End and John O' Groats to be with us. The whole evening was like something out of *This is Your Life* and John and I were choked with emotion having all our pals under one roof. It made us feel very humble and it's an evening I'll never forget. Terry made us stand like newly-weds at the entrance of the suite to greet everybody as they arrived. He'd even arranged for a toastmaster complete with scarlet coat and white gloves and a little hammer to announce them in a booming voice as they walked in. With each new arrival my jaw dropped a little bit further with sheer surprise. Perhaps the biggest one of all came when I saw Stan Webb, now more than eighty years old and my first employer when I was a nanny. The baby I looked after, Sandra, is now grown up and she was there also with her own children. There was one face which looked vaguely familiar and I knew our association stretched back even further, but it wasn't until he said, 'I'm the one with the peanut in my throat, Pol,' that I realized who I was greeting. More than fifty years ago one of the first voices I heard in my ear had saved his life.

At the time Derek Hodson was a baby in his pram. He had suffered a bout of coughing and his distraught mother had started to panic. As Derek turned scarlet a voice had come into my ear and I told her, 'He's got a peanut stuck in his throat.' Now here he was again more than half a century later and, amazingly, a fellow spiritualist. In fact when I gave a demonstration in Nottingham it was Derek who chaired it for me. That ruby wedding party and the reception in this fantastic

216

hotel with all the glittering chandeliers was a far cry from our childhood days in Grantham and yet as I hugged Derek the years rolled back and it seemed as if it had only been yesterday.

Surprise followed surprise. The lovely actress Jean St Clair who overcame her handicap of deafness to star in a West End theatre run *Children of a Lesser God* is another old friend whom Terry invited. There were whole coach loads of people we hadn't seen for years and I have to admit I blinked back more than a few tears as they arrived. To think they had taken all this trouble just for John and I. It was the most incredible night of our lives and even now I don't know how Terry managed it all. He must have been planning it for at least a year beforehand.

He had laid on everything, including a band, and the meal was a banquet fit for a king. I still treasure the menu which was specially printed for us. There was a choice of prawn cocktail or melon with Parma ham followed by roast best end of lamb and a large selection of fresh vegetables and then sherry trifle. And of course there was that sherry reception before we all sat down.

The evening even ended with a surprise when Danny la Rue and his manager Jack popped in to give us a congratulatory hug.

Later as I climbed into bed with the music of the 'Anniversary Waltz' still whirling round inside my head, I thought back over our forty years together. We'd had our ups and downs, but then life would be monotonous if it was all plain sailing, and we'd stuck together through thick and thin. We'd never made a fortune but John and I had something money could never buy. We'd had a full rich and loving life together and along the way we had made some of the best friends in the world.

Chapter Twenty-Two

I never dreamed when I first stepped out onto that stage at the Dominion I would find myself back so soon. Yet here I was once again. Only this time there was a slight difference. Bert Weedon was also going to appear, as was Brendan Blake, an Irishman with a beautiful voice. In the dressing-room with me was Lady Lindsay, an old friend who is probably better remembered as Michaela Denis, who used to star in those big game tv films with her late husband Armand. And in my hand was a cheque for £6,215 raised by all those wonderful people in the audience for the Save the Children Fund.

It was after the first evening at the Dominion that we had the idea to stage a special charity evening for the Fund, but never in my wildest dreams did I think it would be so successful. Bert Weedon, who by this time had become a firm friend, was only too happy to give his services free and we decided that all the money we raised should go to the fund being organized by *Woman's Own*.

It seemed that everyone wanted to help in some way – even the spirit world – and by the evening of the actual demonstration every ticket in the house had been sold.

Ten days earlier I had been sitting in the kitchen talking with John and our friend Nancy and told them, 'Wouldn't it be absolutely marvellous if the first spirit to come through was a child.'

At that moment there was a mischievous voice in

218

my ear. It was young and it had a broad Scottish accent. 'My Mummy and Daddy will be there.' It was a little boy. I could tell that but I certainly wasn't prepared for his next remark. 'Canna have the floo'ers?' For a moment I was puzzled. Then I suddenly realized what he was talking about. At every demonstration I like to give away the flowers on the stage and more often than not they go to the parents of a spirit child who has come through during the evening.

Quite often the spirit children ask me to give the flowers to their mummy or daddy but never before had one made the request ten days in advance of the demonstration. I had to laugh at this young man's determination. He was making sure he got in first.

'Of course you can have the flowers, pet,' I said. 'But I don't even know your name.'

'It's Garry. Garry O'Connell and I lived near Glasgow.' And then he was gone.

John and Nancy could see that I was laughing to myself. They hadn't heard the conversation of course but they realized that something had happened and Nancy said, 'Are you going to share the joke?'

'It isn't really a joke,' I replied. 'I've just got what I think is a contact for our charity evening. And the way he's just been talking I'm willing to bet he'll be the first one through.' And he was, of course.

I had only been on stage for a matter of minutes when that little voice came through again saying, 'Don't forget the floo'ers!'

I could see him quite clearly now. He'd got a dummy in his mouth which was making it even harder to understand Master Garry and he was holding the side of his head.

I asked him as gently as I could, 'What are your parents' names, Garry?'

'Maurice and Jeanette. And then there's Auntie Pat.'

I turned to the audience and asked if there was anybody called O'Connell. From the back of the auditorium came a man's voice. 'Here, Doris!'

'Is your name Maurice?'

'Yes!'

'I thought we couldn't be wrong this evening, luv. And your wife, her name is Jeanette?'

'Yes, I'm here too, Doris!' She was sitting alongside her husband.

'I've got Garry here with me, luv. He's laughing all over his face but he will insist on keeping his dummy in his mouth.'

Jeanette laughed. 'He liked his dummy.'

'He still does,' I replied.

Garry interrupted again saying, 'Don't forget Auntie Pat, don't forget her.'

And sure enough Auntie Pat had come along too. I asked her why Garry had been holding his head when he first appeared. It was because he had died from a brain tumour. But now he had forgotten any pain he might have had. Garry was waving his arms as frantically and energetically as any three-year-old on the earth plane. He was dancing with joy at having made contact with his family for the first time since he had passed over. And he was especially proud that he was first in the queue for the floo'ers which I sent to his parents with Garry's love.

I had a feeling that one or two children would be coming through on this special evening and I was right. As a result we gave away several bouquets of 'floo'ers'!

In all it was a memorable evening and a marvellous

end to the tour. It was also one of the proudest moments of my life when I was able to present Professor Hobbs of Westminster Children's Hospital in London with that cheque.

To everyone who contributed I would like to say God Bless You. But I must admit I was a bit apprehensive.

Professor Hobbs had come along with Iris Burton, editor of *Woman's Own*, which was organizing an appeal on behalf of the Save the Children Fund to raise money for a new bone marrow unit at the hospital. Although our cheque was going towards buying this unit I wasn't sure how the Professor had viewed the evening's proceedings – especially since Bert Weedon had almost brought the house down with 'Ghost Riders in the Sky'. But I needn't have worried. He walked onto the stage, gave me a hug and said, 'Doris, it's a revelation. I've enjoyed myself so much.' And so, I'm pleased to say, had everybody else.

That evening was among the most memorable of the twelve months because it combined two things I love most, doing my job as a medium and helping children, if only in a small way. Throughout my life children have been at the root of my greatest moments of both joy and heartbreak. They have also been a source of inspiration and understanding.

Before I lost John Michael I could meet someone in the street who would tell me tearfully that they had just lost a loved one and I would say, 'Oh, I am sorry for you.' And at that moment I would genuinely mean it. But I could turn the next corner, see a dress in a shop window and say to myself, 'Isn't that nice, I wonder if they've got it in my size?' I would have completely forgotten the suffering I had seen only minutes before. Maybe that's the reaction of any normal young girl and perhaps it's what I've seen and experienced over the years that makes me what I am now. All I know is that these days I can sit at home looking at the photographs of my spirit children as I am doing now and suddenly I'll think of the parents of one of them.

I'll say to myself. 'I wonder how they are coping?' I wonder if the sun has started to shine again for them? Believe me it will. During my thoughts I'll say a little prayer, not down on my knees or with my hands piously clasped together, but just by sending out loving thoughts to the parents and their child. That to me is a prayer and my spirit friends tell me how much it uplifts them just to know we think about them.

Looking at old photographs of close ones who have passed over and remembering them with love is enough. You don't have to make a great show of things, it's what you feel in your heart and what you believe that really counts. I know my mother and father still walk with me. I don't go putting flowers on their graves. I couldn't even tell you in which plot they are buried. They shed their old overcoats the day they went over and I'm not going to make a shrine out of their graves. They are not there. They are with me here and now. A few flowers by their photographs on the anniversary of their passing cheers them up no end.

Everyone should try not to mourn for too long. Have a good old cry by all means. Cry your heart out again and again and try to let the tears wash away your sorrow. It's all part of God's healing process. I know that if I were to lose my beloved John I would weep buckets, but I also know he would be up there doing his darndest to help me sort things out, and that he would be back with me again at my end waiting to take me over and show me that beautiful world on the other side.

My tears would be for the loss of his physical presence, which I would miss more than anything else on this earth. The loneliness and misery at not being able to reach out and touch his hand now and again as we watch television at night, would at first be almost unbearable. But I would have to go through that process of grieving just the same as anyone else, so that the healing process can begin.

I also know however that from the depths of my despair, one day I would wake up and the sun would be shining again. The healing would be complete and I would get on with the job of living.

Cutting someone out of your life is the same as cutting something away from your body. You can never have it back, you can never erase the scar completely and every now and then it hurts – even years afterwards. But slowly the wound heals and, while there will never be perfection, in time the scar doesn't show so much. But we never forget the experience.

I have to admire the dear old lady I read about recently who hired a brass band for her funeral. As her coffin was carried out of the door they played 'Wish Me Luck As You Wave Me Goodbye'. I should think she had a really good chuckle as she looked down on that scene and that's the way it should be, because make no mistake, we can all see our own funeral if we wish. I wouldn't miss mine for all the tea in China. I've already decided what tunes I want playing, and although it won't be Bert Weedon with

'Ghost Riders in the Sky' — it won't be the 'Death March' either.

When and how we pass over, of course, is in the hands of God and although his timing may sometimes seem cruel to us there is a reason that in time we will understand. Meanwhile my rule is to live every day as if it is my last, so that when I am called I can honestly say, 'Dear God, thank you for a rich and full life. And thank you for the gift you gave me. I hope you approve of what I have done with it.'